RED AMARYLLIS

DENISE E. JACOBS

"If you don't believe in an afterlife or higher purpose then Red Amaryllis will make you think again." **- Reader's Digest**

"Red Amaryllis offers an unforgettable, heart-wrenching story of struggle and adversity underpinned by one ordinary woman's extraordinary calling." **- The Scotsman**

"A clarion call for peace, love and understanding but, more importantly, a convincing entreaty for us all to act before it's too late." **- Female First**

"If you have any concerns about where the world is heading then you have to read this book."
- The Yorkshire Post

"After reading this book, even the hardest sceptic would be hard-pressed to deny that Denise E. Jacobs has an uncanny ability to call the future with unnerving accuracy."
- Bucks Herald

"I was left stunned by what I read in Red Amaryllis. While the rational part of me says it can't possibly be true, the evidence is just too compelling to ignore."
- Hastings Observer

"Everyone will be rewarded by reading this unforgettable book, but it's our world leaders who must read it... for all our sakes." **- Lancashire Evening Post**

"Unless we demand that those with power change direction, Jacobs' foreseen horrors will become known to us all" **- Soul & Spirit**

"Red Amaryllis is an astonishing true story of one woman's victory against a financial giant, and the greater battle to come in convincing the world that catastrophe is approaching unless we act now." **- Sheffield Telegraph**

"Memoirs are usually the preserve of the rich and famous, but author Denise E. Jacobs has led such a remarkable life that her true story deserves to be told —and read." **- Derbyshire Times**

"As her sensational true life story attests, author Denise E. Jacobs is a survivor. Now she wants all of humanity to survive by coming together to avert an impending nuclear Armageddon." **- Bedford Today**

"David vs Goliath has nothing on the legal fight that Denise E. Jacobs and her husband took on against a multinational financial company, which ended in miraculous circumstances." **- Coleraine Times**

"Why the title 'Red Amaryllis'? It turns out that this was the author's favourite birthday present from her parents. In writing this stirring memoir, Denise is now passing that gift on to us all." **- Eastbourne Herald**

"The one thing you quickly learn by reading Red Amaryllis is not to bet against author Denise E. Jacobs. A multinational financial firm did, and failed. Now Denise is warning that our world is in peril. Dare we not listen?"
- The News

First published in Great Britain as a softback original in 2021

Copyright © Denise E. Jacobs

The moral right of this author has been asserted.

All rights reserved.

No part of this publication may be reproduced, stored in a retrieval system, or transmitted, in any form or by any means, without the prior permission in writing of the publisher, nor be otherwise circulated in any form of binding or cover other than that in which it is published and without a similar condition including this condition being imposed on the subsequent purchaser.

Published by: Red Amaryllis
Address: PO Box No 1223
Uxbridge Sorting Office
Cowley Road
Uxbridge
Middlesex
UB8 9GN
website: *www.redamaryllis.org*
Twitter: @TheRedAmaryllis

Book cover design by Ivica Jandrijevic

Cover illustration by Henry Relf

Typesetting by UK Book Publishing
www.ukbookpublishing.com

ISBN: 978-1838321505

RED AMARYLLIS

DENISE E. JACOBS

Dear Sir Sydney,

There are no words in the dictionary that are able to thank you enough for all your wise and wonderful advice; and also your kindness to a total stranger. Without you, this book would not have been written.

I send my love to you for all you did.

Denise. xx

For Michael and Daniel.

My gratitude to my knight in shining armour,
Grahame Sutton, without whose help this
book would never have been written.

The only way of discovering the limits of the possible is to venture a little way past them into the impossible

– Arthur C Clark

Everything in this story is true and can be confirmed by witness statements, contemporaneous notes, emails, parliamentary records, court pleadings, sworn affidavits, court transcripts and personal diaries.

The symbolic Doomsday Clock, introduced in 1947, was designed to show how close mankind is to the destruction of our planet by the abuse and misuse of dangerous technologies of our own making.

FOREWORD

Okay ... okay ... I understand. You have read the back cover and have seen that this book's protagonist claims to be able to see the future.

Depending on your level of cynicism, you might even have rolled your eyes.

I understand; I really do because I was just the same as you.

However, I can promise you that the stories printed on these pages will captivate and amaze even the biggest cynics. If, however, the evidence fails to convince you then, at the very least, it is still a great read about a modern-day 'David versus Goliath' court case, with one woman risking everything to challenge one of the world's largest financial institutions. Who knows, it might even make you question your beliefs along the way.

Dan Jacobs

DEAR READER,

How would the people of the world react if they were given proof that those in the next dimension to ours can see our past, present, and future?

Would the world accept it, or turn a blind eye?

Would the leaders of the world try to prove it was a lie?

Would they try to deny it, or ignore it?

Those with a hunger for power will always attempt to cover up the truth.

But what if the key to proving the truth is in this book? What if you, the people of the world, could make up your own minds about the biggest question facing humankind?

It's time to make up your mind.

Are you ready?

What you will learn from this book will change forever the way you see this world... and the next.

And if you're ready to discover the truth from this book, then let me tell you that

there is a great and powerful good to be served, in which you have a vital part to play.

Each one of us must play our part, if we are to save this world of ours.

And time is running out.

Only we can decide our future.

Denise

PROLOGUE

THE MUSHROOM CLOUD

August 28th, 1985

Darlington, Co Durham, England

'Look out of the window.'

Who spoke? I was in the kitchen with my baby son. No-one else there. But I heard a woman's voice, right beside me.

I turned towards the window and froze.

It was a sunny day and the sky outside had been clear blue all morning, but nothing could prepare me for the unimaginable nightmare that was unfolding.

There was a blinding flash of light followed by a deafening boom so loud my eardrums felt as if they'd shattered. I could feel blood ooze from them, my eyes felt swollen and weeping blisters appeared on my body. I put my hands over my face in a futile attempt to stop the excruciating agony. I watched the sky grow dark as the sun was obliterated by a vast, billowing mushroom cloud that rose thousands of feet as it expanded into a mass of smoke and flames and darkness that filled the horizon until it was all I could see; silent, ominous and terrifying.

I was paralysed with terror; I could only watch as men, women, children and babies evaporated before me. Others screamed with the hell of being set on fire. Many turned to ash, while those who survived, desperate for water, turned their open mouths to the sky as large drops of poisonous black rain fell on them. The more they swallowed, the more intense their thirst became. I felt bile rising in my throat as I tried to assimilate the horror of what I had witnessed.

"What is this?" I whispered.

As fast as it had appeared, the view outside my window became clear and sunny once more. Shaken and dazed, it was a moment before I remembered my son, Daniel. He had been strangely quiet and now he sat motionless in his highchair, his eyes fixed on me.

I felt sick. I knew I had just been shown something momentous and utterly terrifying.

Then I heard her voice again.

"You are looking at the future. Nuclear war is coming if the world does not change the course it is on, and it will affect every single person on the planet as well as those who are to come in future generations. From where I am, we can see the past, the present and the future, but we can't change what is coming; we can only warn you. We need you to help us get this message through to the people of the world because only they can demand peace, and put an end to the madness of power-hungry leaders who think that war is the answer. Your journey will be long and difficult, but we will be here to help you."

What was she talking about? Me? Help stop nuclear war?

The whole thing sounded crazy. All I knew was that I would never, ever forget the sight of that terrible mushroom cloud; it would haunt me for as long as I lived.

In contrast to the happy soul I was moments earlier, I felt as though the weight of the world was now on my shoulders. Was the unthinkable going to happen? Or was this all just a monstrous vision? I was confused, scared and eaten up with worry at what I had seen, and I couldn't get the images out of my head.

That day marked a defining moment. My life had been changed forever, and deep down I knew it. I didn't want to see the destruction of our world, or to have to spend my life working to prevent it. I didn't want to be chosen for a task that seemed enormous and impossible.

The trouble was – I knew that I had no choice.

1947

7 MINUTES TO MIDNIGHT

Initial setting of the Doomsday Clock

Estimated number of nuclear
warheads worldwide:

13

CHAPTER ONE

THE FLOWER SELLER

November 12th, 2013

The Flower Stall, Uxbridge
Underground Station, London

The flower seller was walking away, but then stopped in his tracks before turning towards the corner of his stall, where he reached down and scooped two large bunches of blooms from a bucket. Deftly, he wrapped them and walked over to me and put the flowers into my arms.

"Here you go love, have some flowers on me."

As I looked down at the flowers, I heard my father's voice, just behind me.

"Happy Birthday, Denise. These are for you, with love from Dad and Mum."

"Thank you so much," I said to the flower seller. The flowers were wrapped up so tightly that I couldn't see what they were.

"What are they?" I asked.

"Amaryllises," he replied, "otherwise known in Latin as Hippeastrum. In Greek it means 'to sparkle'."

He leaned closer to me and whispered. "To be honest, this is a first. If I gave every customer free flowers I'd go bust, so this is between you and me, okay love?"

"Of course," I said. My throat felt so constricted that I was sure my voice must sound odd. "Can I ask, are they... red?"

"Yes, matter of fact they are," he grinned.

His words faded as I heard my father's voice again. I repeated what he was saying to me. "There weren't any white ones at the wholesalers this morning, only red."

The flower seller looked dumbfounded. "That's right; how the heck did you know that?" He leaned towards me, looking concerned. "Are you alright? You look a bit pale."

I stood rooted to the spot, staring at the stems that I knew would open into the stunning rich red of the amaryllis blooms I loved so much, struggling to take in what was happening.

I looked up at him.

"It's my birthday today, and it was a birthday tradition that my parents gave me red amaryllises every year. It started when I was young, but I didn't think it would be remotely possible for it to happen this year."

"Why not?" he asked.

"Because both my parents died in the last month, within days of one another. This morning I thought of them and wondered whether they knew what day it was.

Now I know they do."

****

As my husband, Michael drove me home, tears rolled down my cheeks. Finally, after all the years that had passed and all the heartache, loss and grief I had been through, everything fell into place. My parents' gift to me was the final confirmation I needed – it was like the last piece in a huge jigsaw. They had reached the world that I knew to be inter-connected with this one, and they had sent me a powerful message. In life, they had sometimes doubted me, but now they were telling me that they knew the truth and they wanted me to act.

When we got home, I put the amaryllises into a large vase in the middle of our dining table. As I looked at them, I understood that it made sense to prove it to me this way, with a tender, loving gesture to let me know that, like the other souls in the next dimension, my parents wanted to warn us that we are heading towards a terrifying future.

A future that is individually and collectively in our power to change.

For 30 years, since I first saw that first extraordinary image of a nuclear explosion, I had been given signs, messages and warnings. I had been told of tasks that I had to complete, and sent along a path that appeared to be uncertain and filled with hardship. Many times I had doubted, or felt that I couldn't go on. But whenever I did, I was directed towards my next step. Sometimes I had been given messages that took my breath away and proved to me yet again, beyond doubt, that those in the next dimension knew what I did not, and that I had to trust in them and carry on.

Along the way I was able to help many other people, enabling them to connect with those they had lost and to make life-changing decisions. I came to understand that every single piece of information I was given, no matter how minor or how unconnected it might appear, was for one single purpose – to help me to find a way to prevent the nuclear Armageddon looming ahead of us.

Since World War Two, bigger and bigger nuclear devices had been developed, hundreds of times more powerful than the bomb that was dropped on Hiroshima in 1945. By the time my parents sent me the amaryllises for my birthday, in 2013, there were thousands of these enormous nuclear weapons pointing at every one of us in this beautiful world of ours. It would only take one egotistical man or woman with an itchy trigger finger to start the countdown to extinction. The clock was ticking, and I knew it was time to act.

Before I explain what lies ahead for us all if we don't stop the nuclear war that is coming in just a few years' time, let me first go back to the beginning of what has been an extraordinary journey. I want to tell you the tale of what happened to me and how it happened, because the story is so much a part of the message.

I'd always thought that people who were psychic knew it from early childhood. I'd read stories of 'gifted' youngsters who 'knew' things they couldn't have known, or who received 'special' messages from voices they alone could hear.

Well, that wasn't me. I was an ordinary girl from Darlington, a small town in the north-east of England. I was quiet and shy and happy to go through life blending in with the crowd. So when, in my twenties, my life started to change in extraordinary ways, I felt as though I'd somehow got onto a merry-go-round that was spinning faster and faster, with no way to get off.

It began one day when I started to feel very strange sensations. My heart started racing and I felt detached from reality, while in my mind's eye I saw an image of a car accident. Simultaneously there was an intense pulsating in my solar plexus; that spot in the centre of the abdomen, between the ribs, and I felt a sense of acute urgency, a bit like the feeling you get when you know something you're cooking is about to burn, and you have to stop what you're doing and run to save it.

The whole experience passed in a flash. It was extraordinary and it left me alarmed and worried because I felt absolutely sure that the car I'd seen was my father's, and that he was going to have a car accident the following day. I phoned to tell him and begged him to be careful, but of course he laughed at the idea that I could know such an event was coming, especially as he was a careful driver and very protective of his car.

"Ring me tomorrow and let me know you're OK, anyway," I said, and he promised he would.

He phoned the next morning to say all was well, then phoned me again several times during the day. "No accident Denise, I'm fine," he said. His last call was at 10pm to say he was going to bed. "Sorry Denise, it didn't happen. Never mind." I was relieved – of course I was – but I was puzzled too because it had seemed so clear. Had I made a mistake?

The following morning Dad phoned me. "You'll never believe this, but at 11.30 last night the police called to say that the alarm was ringing at your mother's hair salon. I had to get out of bed and drive down there to see what was going on. It was a false alarm, but as I was leaving the car park, some idiot reversed into my car."

"What time did it happen, Dad?"

He laughed. "It was just before midnight. So you were right

after all."

Thankfully, the accident was minor, Dad was fine, and his car could be fixed. But I had accurately predicted the accident. Dad was stunned, and so was I. Michael stuck to his non-believer guns and said, "It was just a lucky guess." But it was not a guess at all; I had known what would happen. What I didn't yet understand was why or how I had known.

A few weeks later, my brother Terry and his wife Sandra invited us to dinner with several other couples. We were all sitting around the dining room table after the meal when Terry mentioned that I'd predicted Dad's car accident. One of the women was intrigued, but her husband scoffed at the idea.

"Prove it to us," everyone laughingly insisted. And a few moments later I began to have the same strange sensations I'd had when I saw Dad's car accident. It was as though a different part of my brain took over.

I looked at Terry and blurted out, "You're having an affair with someone!" Everyone roared with laughter, but Terry looked furious. "Don't be so bloody ridiculous Denise, of course I'm not. What rubbish!" he responded followed by nervous laughter. My goodness, the next few moments in that room were awkward. He sprang up from the table and marched out of the room. Meanwhile one of the other guests, Pru, took a few large gulps of wine as her chest turned a bright shade of red that gradually spread upward to her face.

I was mortified by what I'd said – it had just popped out before I'd got my brain in gear to stop myself. At least Sandra hadn't been in the room. I followed Terry, apologising. He turned to me and said loudly, "Well, you didn't get that one right." Then he hissed, "You're right, but you have to stop. I'll explain it all later." Those weren't the only words he said to me in private, but I dare not print them because they are far too profane!

The party soon broke up, and Michael and I went home. "What were you thinking, coming out with that?" he said.

"I don't know," I replied miserably. "I just had this weird sensation and I had to say it."

Michael laughed. "As if Terry would be having an affair."

I looked at him. "But he is. He told me later that he was. I shouldn't have come out with it like that, but it was true."

The following day, Terry came over to see me. "The honest truth – I don't know how you knew, but I've been seeing Pru for the last few months. She was horrified when you said it – her husband was next to me, laughing. The last thing I want is for him or Sandra to find out."

I apologised and told Terry I hadn't meant to upset anyone, although he did need to sort out his private life. Sandra was never very friendly to me, but I was still upset to think that he was seeing someone else behind her back.

After that, I promised myself that I would be careful about what I said in public. The last thing I wanted was to hurt anyone or cause problems. But I couldn't help being thrilled that I'd been right, although I still wasn't sure how I'd managed it. Would it happen again? I had no idea.

1949

3 MINUTES TO MIDNIGHT

Soviet Union performs its first nuclear tests

Estimated number of nuclear
warheads worldwide:

171

CHAPTER TWO

YOU HAVE THE GIFT

Darlington, 1982 - 1983

"We can't talk to dead people. It's not possible. When you're dead, you're dead... end of."

"Do you really think so?" I asked.

I was still feeling shaken after all that had happened, and we were debating the possibility of an after-life and whether psychics were just a bunch of con merchants.

"Yes!" Michael said emphatically. "It's conceit, or wishful thinking, to believe that there's anything more after we pop our clogs."

I was inclined to agree with him; I usually trusted his judgment. By this time we had been married for over ten years. We had our own hair salon and a good life, with family and friends around us. And despite being different in many ways, we loved one another very much. Our life was pretty simple and straightforward, and I wanted it to stay that way.

Except that it didn't. Over the next few weeks I began

to feel very strange. Something was happening to me, and I really didn't know how to cope with it. I felt a curious pain in my solar plexus; sometimes it felt like an ache, and at other times it felt like the butterflies you get when you're nervous. And there were moments when I felt as if something was nagging at me, or someone was trying to get my attention.

My skin became sensitive and started to tingle, a bit like the hairs on the back of your neck or the goosebumps you get when you see a horror movie. My sense of smell and hearing increased, so much so that any loud noise, even laughter, hurt my ears. And without intending or wanting to, I was tuning into others' emotions; if people were sad, I felt it so deeply that I wanted to cry with them. It was all strange, extremely uncomfortable and unsettling and I had no idea what it meant.

Then came the next dinner party fiasco. Darlington was a small place where everyone knew everyone else and we often had these dinners, rotating between our homes. This time we were at Terry and Sandra's again and there were about ten of us around the table. Sandra was serving French bread and baked brie (this was the 70s), the wine flowed and there was a lot of talk and laughter.

I was very quiet. This wasn't unusual for me; I was shy and found it difficult to jump into conversations. But this particular night it was more than just my usual reticence – I found the noise around me almost unbearable and my solar plexus was in huge discomfort. It was as if I was picking up the feelings of everyone there. By the time the main course arrived I couldn't take any more; I put my hands over my ears, desperate to shut out the shrieking cacophony surrounding me.

"You alright?" Michael asked.

"No, I need to go home," I whispered.

"Sorry, but Denise isn't well," Michael told everyone as he took my hand and led me out.

The relief when we got outside was enormous. "What's going on with you?" Michael asked. "I don't know," I said. Michael was worried, and so was Terry, who came round the next day to see if I was alright. "You looked as white as a sheet when you left," he said.

"I'm sorry for spoiling your party," I told him. "I felt weird, like my skin was crawling and sounds and smells were unbearable." Terry was sympathetic, but just like me and Michael, he was mystified.

I felt I was drowning in the middle of a maelstrom of noise, sound and emotion every time I left the house and I had no idea where to turn. I was desperate for it all to stop.

Michael was looking for a solution too, and when he read in the paper about an evening of clairvoyance, he decided we should go. "It might help shed some light on what your over-active imagination is doing to you," he said cheerfully.

Mum and Dad were having a party on the same night. We went around to my parents' house at 5.30 and prepared the dinner, as Mum had requested, but when she got home from work Michael told her that we weren't going to stay because we were off to see a medium. Used to getting her own way, Mum was furious. "You're dealing with the devil and if that's what you want to do you will never be welcome in my house again," she shouted. Dad, while not as vocal, wasn't happy either. I wavered, but Michael was used to dealing with my parents' upsets and he calmly replied that it was settled, we were going, before marching me out of the door.

At the entrance of the small wood-panelled hall where the meeting was to be held two women sat selling tickets. They both stared at me for several seconds, making me blush to my hairline. "Hello," one of them said. "We've been expecting you." The other one nodded in agreement and smiled. I was startled; had they confused me with someone else?

On the other side of a heavy red velvet curtain was a crowded hall. We edged our way to two empty seats in the middle of the back row just as a woman on the small stage was welcoming the audience. Shortly afterwards I felt a very odd sensation in my solar plexus. It didn't feel scary, in fact it was quite the opposite; more like an overwhelming feeling of pure love. As rays of yellow light formed around the woman on the stage, I blinked. The light seemed to be radiating from her and I could see it extending out through the wall behind her, into the far distance. It was the most mesmerising, luminous and extraordinary light I had ever seen. As I looked at it, captivated, I understood that this light was the connection between us and the souls who have passed on from this life.

At that moment the woman pointed to me.

"You have the gift of being able to communicate with those who have departed this world and moved into the next dimension." I looked around. "Yes, you, dear – it's you I'm talking to," she said, looking straight at me. "Strange things have been happening to you and you need to learn how to handle it."

I was dumbfounded. Then she pointed at Michael. "You will come up with a business idea and it will be for a very special reason. Because of this, no matter how hard it may become, you must keep going with it."

Michael and I sat open-mouthed at what she had said as

she spoke in turn to various audience members. Were the strange feelings and sensations I'd been experiencing really to do with me developing some kind of psychic ability?

At home, we sat at the kitchen table with mugs of tea, talking about what had just happened. "I don't know about you being psychic," Michael said. "It seems pretty potty to me. As for what she said to me, what kind of business idea would I have? I'm a hairdresser, not a businessman. And what's the special reason?"

"I have no idea," I said. "I guess we'll have to wait for the answers."

I decided to attend a meeting of the local psychic group. If the medium was right that I was psychic, then perhaps they could help me with the sensations and feelings I was having. So a couple of weeks later, back I went to the little hall, where the psychic group welcomed me warmly.

During the meeting they explained more about how to access our inner psychic powers. I was told to close my eyes and look for the 'third eye' – the invisible eye, traditionally placed in the centre of the forehead, that many believe provides perception beyond ordinary sight. They said I should look for a pin-prick of light above my forehead. I tried hard to concentrate and eventually I did see a little white dot in the darkness. Next, I was encouraged to look for symbols. For a while nothing happened, but then I started to see a very quick flash of something white.

I went back for more sessions and, frustrated that nothing was clear, tried repeatedly to relax and concentrate. During one session, I saw a bar of chocolate floating around and I had a sense that it related to the woman next to me. I turned to her. "Are you addicted to chocolate?" I asked. "I am," she grinned. Then a name popped into my head, "Is your name Sue?" "Yes," she replied. I grinned like a Cheshire cat.

A bar of chocolate might not have seemed like the most exciting start, but to me just getting a clear symbol was thrilling, and it encouraged me to keep on trying. Eventually, with my eyes squeezed shut and concentrating as hard as I could, I started to see more symbols and to work out what they meant.

Gradually I learned how to join one symbol to another until I was able to pass on to the recipients what I had seen. At one point early on, I saw a pair of scissors and I felt sure it meant the end of a relationship. I said that to the person next to me and she confirmed she had just finished with her boyfriend. She was amazed, and so was I.

Why me? I wondered. I felt overwhelmed by the idea. One of the psychics running the group told me, "You may not be keen on the idea of getting messages from the other side, but you are particularly sensitive to it".

Soon after this Michael had a phone call to say that his father was in hospital after a heart attack. He was stable, but we needed to go and see him. Michael was an only child and his mother had died three years earlier, so his father was alone.

We headed straight down to London by train, and then hopped into a taxi to take us to the hospital. When the taxi hit a major traffic jam, sitting beside me in the back, restless and bored, Michael said, "If only I could watch Coronation Street right here in the taxi."

I looked at him as awareness dawned on me. "That's it, Michael, that's the idea!"

"What do you mean?" he said.

"You were told you would have a business idea, and here it is – screens in the backs of taxis."

"Do you think so?" he said. "I was just having a laugh really, thinking how nice it would be to have a telly here."

"I feel certain this is it," I said. "Imagine if it was a reality – every taxi would want to carry one. And what about planes, trains and buses too? The possibilities are huge. They could run videos of films and TV shows, perhaps even guides to the places you're visiting."

"I can see what you mean," he said. "But how on earth would we get that to happen? Who would pay for the screens and the videos?"

"Advertisers," I said, beginning to get excited. "If it worked, they'd have a captive audience, wouldn't they?"

"Mmm, perhaps we really are onto something."

"We can talk about it later," I said, as the taxi started to move. "First let's go and see how your dad is."

Michael's father was happy to see us. It wasn't easy for him, living so far from his only son. He was out of danger and would be sent home soon, and we promised to stay for a few days.

Back in the flat where Michael had grown up and where his father still lived, we talked over the idea of screens in cabs and planes. Michael was still unsure, but I felt sure that this was the idea we'd been told about. Eventually he agreed to look into it.

"I guess it can't hurt," he said. "Dad always worked as a salesman for other people. He never took any chances in life or did anything adventurous. So maybe I should. If I try and fail, well, at least I'll have had a go."

It wasn't the most inspiring of start-up speeches, but I was touched. He was making a bold decision, under duress from me, and he was right – we weren't business people. It would take us out of our comfort zone into the unknown.

The next day we went to the Hackney Carriage Office on the Holloway Road. When we got there, we told the man in charge about our idea and he said he'd need to see a prototype cab, with the screen fitted.

A few days later, with Michael's father back at home and doing well, we headed home and started researching ways to make this new business idea happen. My father was an engineering draughtsman, so we asked him if he could help us to get the idea up and running. He had a strong entrepreneurial spirit and could never resist a challenge, so he said yes.

After that, we worked in the salon by day and on the development by night. Michael worked out the demographics and costings and we prepared brochures and sales and marketing leaflets.

In the middle of all this, in the spring of 1983, we had a wonderful surprise – I found out I was pregnant, and the baby was due in December. For the next few months, I continued hairdressing and researching the new video idea while riding the wave of all the early pregnancy symptoms, from nausea to strange aches and pains and weird food cravings.

We managed to buy a third-hand black Hackney carriage in Birmingham and began working on a way to fit a screen in the back, which turned out to be more complicated than we thought. In the meantime, Michael and I travelled the length and breadth of the UK in the cab, visiting councils to see if they'd come on board with the idea. The taxi had no power steering and the heater couldn't be switched off, so travelling in it was pretty grim. I sat in the back, throwing up constantly, while Michael drove. We visited Glasgow, Edinburgh, Birmingham, Manchester, Blackpool and Liverpool, getting agreements to operate in those cities. London was waiting to see how well the electronics worked before allowing us in.

We registered the company as Transport Media (Great Britain) Ltd, trading as Videocab. Worldwide patents were put in place and we even flew to New York to discuss the idea with the taxi commissioner, who gave us a conditional agreement to install TV's in yellow cabs once we knew how it was going to work.

It was exciting and terrifying. We could make our fortune – or lose everything. The psychic had not said whether the business would work or not, she had simply said that it would be for a reason. What that was, we still didn't know.

A couple of months before the baby was due, we were at another of our dinner get-togethers. "When do you think your baby will be born, Sis?" Terry asked me.

The doctor had told me that the baby was due on New Year's Eve. But just as I knew my father would have his car accident and Terry was having an affair, I had the same strange but certain feeling that the medical team had it wrong.

"I'm convinced the birth will be on Christmas Day. I think it's going to be between midnight and two in the morning." The room fell silent as every pair of eyes turned towards me.

"Come off it, I bet you a quid you're wrong," Michael exclaimed.

"Can we all have bets too?" came the chorus from the others around the table.

Late on Christmas Eve I began to feel some discomfort. Unsure what was going on, I phoned the hospital and was told to come in. As I put the phone down, Michael said, "If you have that baby between midnight and 2am, not only will I lose my quid but I'll have to believe elephants really can fly."

We headed to North Tees Hospital where I was greeted by Dr Brown, the obstetrician, who was wearing a bright green satin bowtie with banana yellow dots. After hooking me up to a monitor, he announced, "All the readings show you're not in labour – so you may as well go home."

"I think the contractions have started," I said.

"Denise, nothing is showing up on the monitor." Dr Brown was clearly keen to go home. He had no idea that the monitor wasn't working – something that was only discovered later. In the corridor outside my room, I could hear *Rudolf the Red Nose Reindeer* at full throttle as I explained, through gritted teeth, that the contractions were becoming stronger.

Still insisting that nothing was happening, Dr Brown, along with the midwife, who happened to be Mrs Brown, wished everyone a Merry Christmas and hurried away, having instructed the nurse to keep me in until the following morning, just to be safe. Michael was told to go home, but he refused to leave, informing the ward sister that the baby would be born between midnight and 2am. "You'd better be right, otherwise I'm going to look a complete idiot," he whispered to me as he went off to find a cup of tea.

Not long after that, my waters broke and the ward sister went to tell Michael that I was now in labour. It was 1am. He gave her an I-told-you-so smile and sprinted to the delivery room where he found me, high as a kite on gas and air.

At 1.15am Team Brown reappeared, and at 1.34 baby Daniel was born.

The nursing staff bolted for the telephones. "North Tees

Hospital here, 1.34am – can you beat that?" There was a competition among all the hospitals in the North East to see which would have the first Christmas Day baby and we won. Daniel was placed in a lace covered crib and dozens of visitors and staff came to see him and left him silver coins. He and I had our picture taken for the papers.

Finally, we were able to take Dan home and start life as a family. As I laid him in his crib, I gazed at my precious son. "What will your future hold, baby Dan?" I whispered as I kissed his head. "Whatever it is, I promise I'll do everything I can to protect you."

1953

2 MINUTES TO MIDNIGHT

The United States tests its first hydrogen bomb

Estimated number of nuclear
warheads worldwide:

1290

CHAPTER THREE

DENISE, CAN YOU HEAR ME?

Darlington 1984

With Michael not due home for an hour, I strapped seven-month-old Dan into his bouncy chair beside me while I sank gratefully into a bath full of bubbles. I closed my eyes, took a deep breath and listened to the wind rustling the leaves of the trees outside the open window.

The peace was broken by a male voice calling my name. My eyes shot open and I listened intently. Nothing. Then I heard the voice again: "Denise, move the pitcher and bowl before Daniel hurts himself."

"Michael, is that you?" I called. I looked at Dan, who was as quiet as a mouse, "Did you hear Daddy?"

Suddenly I felt a strong sense in my solar plexus – stronger than anything I'd ever felt before. I began to breathe more rapidly and my heart pounded. A faint radiance began to fill the room, a pale-yellow glow that danced and shimmered from ceiling to floor and wall to wall. I blinked and rubbed my eyes. What was happening? Then the voice spoke again. "Move the china, right now Denise."

Uneasily, I looked around. There was a decorative old-fashioned pitcher and bowl on the floor – did he mean those? I got out of the bath, grabbed my bathrobe and went to the window to check if Michael's car was parked outside. It wasn't. I shut the window and locked it, as Daniel started to cry. To distract him I sat him on the floor, handing him his favourite toy. I went out to the hallway and looked over the banister, calling, "Michael, is that you? We're upstairs in the bathroom." But there was only the faint sound of the wind outside.

The silence was broken by a crash from the bathroom and a wail from Daniel. Rushing back in I found him surrounded by shards of china from the broken pitcher, holding up his blood-soaked hand. Somehow, he had managed to wriggle across the floor to where the china stood. I swept him into my arms, just as the front door slammed and Michael shouted, "Daddy's home". Hearing Daniel's screams he took the stairs two at a time. Thankfully the cut was only a small one. Michael put a plaster on Dan's finger and his sobs subsided as he examined this interesting new addition to his hand.

A moment later I heard the same male voice, "Denise, can you hear me? Tell Michael I'm his Grandpa Jack."

I turned to Michael, "Was your grandpa called Jack?"

Michael gave me a look, "Yes, he died years ago."

"Tell him I used to be a boxer and I worked at the Royal Mint," the voice said.

I repeated the words to Michael, who replied, "Yes, that's right. How on earth do you know that?"

"Jack's here, in the room with us, he's just told me," I answered. He told me he was thrilled that he was buried with a family photograph in his pocket and asked me to thank Michael's father for putting it there.

"I remember Dad telling me he did that," Michael replied, looking perplexed.

The yellow haze disappeared as quickly as it had arrived. "You look as if you've just seen a ghost," Michael quipped, lifting Dan out of my arms.

"Not seen, heard," I said. "Do you think I'm losing my mind?"

"No. At least I hope not, but I'm not sure how you know any of that because I've never told you much about Jack." This was true – Michael never knew his father's family well.

"He was here," I said. "I told you, he was in the room with us. I heard him as clear as day. I thought it was you talking to me at first. You do believe me, don't you?"

Michael nodded cautiously.

"Before you came home, Jack warned me about Dan and the china; I didn't listen, and look what happened."

For a second, we both stood in silence. "How did your grandfather know what was going to happen in the future? He warned me more than once." I looked up at Michael. "Do you realise what this means? From the dimension where he is now, they can see our future."

Over the days that followed, I thought a lot about Jack's visit and what it might mean. Whatever this was about, I was too far in to stop now, so I decided to work hard on fine-tuning my psychic skills. I wanted to know what was coming next and why I'd been given this ability. I wanted to know what it means to be human, and how life and death work. Whether I would find the answers, only time would tell.

I spent many hours concentrating on using all my senses;

seeing, hearing, smelling, touching and tasting. I began to receive more and more information, which I had to learn to interpret. For instance, I might see a certain car in my mind. I might then see, or sense, its colour. I might feel myself either sitting in the passenger seat or driving the car or simply looking at it.

The next step was interpreting the message – who was it for and what was it about? I knew I was being given these messages and sometimes I was able to ask for clarification; for instance, how many people were in the car. Then I would wait for the next image, giving me the answer, or I could hold up a number of fingers and say, "Is this right?"

After that, I had to find out where the car was going. I might see a row of shops, or the carwash, or the motorway to Scotland and an image of a hotel. If I felt happy and warm in my solar plexus or in my heart, I knew it was a lovely thing that was going to happen. Sometimes I would feel myself flying backwards or forwards in time and I would have to work out how many hours, days, weeks, months, or years were involved. I couldn't always work out all the answers, but I began to understand that if I wasn't given information, it was because I wasn't meant to know.

Receiving information like this could go on for quite a while, and I would be exhausted by the end of a session. But I also felt that I was discovering a whole new dimension of existence. I was definitely learning how to receive and understand information and how to pass it on.

On one occasion we were in a restaurant sitting at a table beside a young couple. There was a lot of noise as the place was packed, but I overheard the woman saying to the man that she was seeing two men and she wasn't sure which to choose.

I was getting messages, so I began to concentrate. I kept looking at the couple, but Michael talking and the waiter coming to take orders distracted me. I realised I had to learn how to shut out all the noise and chatter around me and keep the link going.

As the information came through, I turned to the girl and said, "Excuse me for interrupting, but it's the Gemini man you should commit to." She looked startled. "It's not actually you I want to speak to," I continued. "It's your brother."

Turning to the young man with her, I said, "You've been very depressed recently and you have seriously considered committing suicide, but I want you to know that things will turn out fine and there is a bright future for you." He visibly lightened and thanked me. The girl thanked me too, saying, "I don't know how you knew, but I am going out with a Gemini man and it's true that my brother has been very depressed".

"How did you know all that?" Michael asked me, as we walked back.

"I can't explain it, I just did," I said. "I was given the information; I don't know who it came from."

The months of practise were beginning to pay off. I'd been able to pass on genuinely helpful messages that would affect the future course of these two young people's lives. While I hadn't suddenly become a confident person, being able to do this had allowed me to put aside my usual reticence and speak to strangers in a restaurant. What was happening was making me braver.

I could never tell when a message would be given to me. I had no choice about when or where or who, it would simply happen. One day, with Daniel in his pushchair, I called into a local shop called *Just a Fiver*.

Sifting through the rails for a new pair of jeans, I noticed the manager, Bill Blass, who I knew. My solar plexus was in overdrive and, as I reached him, I heard a voice telling me that he was about to leave this job and move to London, that he was going to change his career from retail fashion to electronics. I told him this, and Bill pulled me to one side and whispered, "How do you know about me moving to London? Nobody knows yet."

"I just... know," I explained, trailing off. Bill looked puzzled. "Well, I am going to London, but I'm definitely not planning anything involving electronics. I'm setting up my own fashion business there."

Red-faced, I insisted, "Bill, you're not going into fashion, you are going into electronics."

He laughed, but some time later I heard that Bill had gone to London. Things with the fashion business hadn't worked out, but he had bumped into someone who offered him a job in computers, which gave him a very happy second career.

What was happening didn't fit with the way Michael saw the world, and yet it was going on right in front of him – and gradually he was coming to accept it. He could see the change in me when I was receiving a message, the way my eyes would glaze over, and he knew that I was telling people accurate things that I couldn't possibly know about them.

My brothers were also very supportive. I was the middle child – Terry was four years older and Paul was five years younger. Terry was very protective of me; I looked up to him and adored him, and we both doted on Paul.

If it wasn't for Terry, I wouldn't be here today. We were on holiday when I was eight and I was swimming in the sea when a motorboat veered too close, causing me to swallow gulps of seawater in its wake. I began to be sick and tried to stand on the seabed, only to realise I was way out of my depth. As I panicked, I went under. I remember seeing bright coloured lights twinkling and then nothing, until a hand grabbed my hair and dragged me to the surface. My big brother saved my life.

Terry left school and went to work in Mum's salon as a hairdresser, but he hated being told what to do, so our parents loaned him the money for his own salon in Thornaby, a few miles from Darlington. In the early 70s he met and married Sandra, and by the time I had Dan they had a daughter, followed by twins, a girl and a boy.

As for Paul, our baby brother was the most gentle, generous and thoughtful person in the universe. He was a real joker; his hobby was magic, and he would practise constantly until he got his latest trick right. He had his own yellow clown outfit, complete with massive ruffle around his neck, a huge yellow wig and big red nose. I named him PB the Clown, and it stuck. He would practise on me after school and at weekends, and when he grew up, he joined the Magic Circle. He would entertain everyone at Dan's birthday parties.

Paul worked in a Wimpy Bar after leaving school before joining Polycell, first in Darlington, and then London. But London was exciting, and Paul moved quickly into the fashion industry.

I spoke to my brothers often and we met up whenever we could, to swap stories, laugh and generally put the world to rights. Both of them accepted my growing ability and believed in me and I was grateful, because my parents regarded the idea of me being psychic as ludicrous; they were hoping I would soon come to my senses and forget "all this nonsense".

In October 1984, three months after Michael's grandfather

Jack spoke to me, I saw a news report on the Ethiopian famine. It was caused by drought, but also violence and human rights abuses by a repressive government. I wanted to sob in despair at all the suffering and poverty. It was all so cruel and senseless.

Watching on the kitchen TV, I asked out loud, "Why are we here? What's the purpose of our existence? Are our lives mapped out? And if they are, can we do anything to change them?"

I didn't expect any answers, but I began to feel that strange nagging feeling in my solar plexus. I knew someone was standing next to me, and I could smell the familiar scent of Ma Griffe perfume. I was terrified that if I moved I would lose the connection, so I remained perfectly still, hardly daring to breathe. The woman seemed almost to inhabit me; I looked down at my hands and could see that they weren't mine, they were chubby with orange nail varnish.

A moment later, I was sitting in an open-topped carriage, on a railway track. I felt the train shudder as it took off at speed, the wind in my hair. I could see the track stretch out before me into the distance. Without warning, the carriage came to an abrupt halt at a junction that was signposted in two directions.

As I looked at the sign, I knew I was being shown how our life works; we are set on our own individual track and we have choices to make every time we encounter a crossroads. Our choices, the way we live our lives and how we treat other people determines our route and what we encounter.

We are all here to learn from our individual experiences. It was suddenly so clear to me that it was mind-blowing.

The woman whose presence I could sense, was full of

heartfelt sympathy and compassion. She said that, as we progress through our lives, we earn our colours from the way we choose to live and what we do in life, be it wrong and bad or right and good. Not only will our actions affect ourselves, but their consequences will affect the lives of those we meet and those we don't, creating a ripple effect, like a pebble in a pond. And we all have to come back and put right whatever we may have done wrong such as inflicting pain and suffering on others, until we understand the meaning of unconditional love and are able to give it.

As I struggled to absorb all that I was being told, the woman said, "Put your hand over your solar plexus, Denise, and then concentrate really hard. Can you feel it?" I did, and it felt so powerful that it actually seemed to pulsate.

"That's your soul," she said. "The colours of your rainbow shine from it, but cannot be seen by the human eye. In time, I will teach you how to see them and interpret them. Each colour has a different meaning and a different consequence.

"When we leave this world for the next dimension, that is what we take with us. Our soul leaves our physical body behind, taking with it all it has learned and earned, from the way you have lived your life, ready for its next journey along the track, which will, if necessary, be one of making amends. It is a never-ending journey for us all."

"What does that mean?" I asked.

"Remember the two caterpillars?" the woman asked.

I recalled a story I loved so much, of the two caterpillars who were so close. When one caterpillar died, the other was devastated and began a vigil beside its body. Days later the caterpillar looked up to see a beautiful butterfly who asked him why he was sobbing. "My best friend died," the caterpillar replied. "But I *am* your best friend," the butterfly explained. "I'm still here."

"There will never be a time when we do not exist," she said.

What did she mean by that? Do we all continue to return forever? How does it all work? I wanted to ask her so many questions. But she had disappeared.

For the first time I understood that we are here to learn and grow. It is all about the choices we make and the way we treat others. We love to say: "What goes around comes around," and I was being told that this is in fact true.

I was drained by the emotion I had experienced. The connection had been unexpected and extraordinary and focusing in such depth took a vast amount of energy. I sat quietly for the next few minutes, trying to take it all in.

It wasn't just that I had received a life-changing message, or that I had made a connection. There was something more. I knew the woman who had contacted me. I knew her well. I knew her voice, I recognised her perfume and her large presence, and I had seen her hands, with their familiar orange nail varnish when I looked down at my own. She had died four years earlier, but before that she had been a big part of my life.

It was Michael's mother, Celia.

1960

7 MINUTES TO MIDNIGHT

Increased cooperation between the United States & the Soviet Union

Estimated number of nuclear warheads worldwide:

20,370

CHAPTER FOUR

CELIA

Mallorca and London 1972-1980

Celia had been a huge personality; larger than life, and very sociable, she talked constantly over everyone and was the absolute opposite of me in almost every way.

Strangely, I wasn't surprised that it was Celia who had made contact with me. Somehow it seemed to fit with who she had been in life. But if I was happy to accept that she had made the connection, Michael was not. When I told him his mother had been with me in the kitchen, he was furious. "Don't be so bloody ridiculous," he said. "Mum's gone, and that's that."

I knew I wasn't going to persuade him, so I left the subject alone. In any case, I needed to take time to think it over.

I had first met Celia after a whirlwind holiday romance in Mallorca with her son. Michael had gone away for two weeks with his childhood friend Dave and come back with a 19-year-old fiancée who wouldn't say boo to a goose. Celia, presented with a fait accompli, took it well. She looked me up and down, gave me a hug and welcomed me into her family.

I had gone on holiday with my parents and 14-year-old Paul. At the weekly dinner dance Michael walked over to our table and asked my parents if he could dance with me. They said yes, but I wasn't happy – since no-one had actually asked *me* if I wanted to dance with this lanky stranger.

At six-foot three he towered over my five-foot three-inch frame. And at 29 he was ten years older than me and he oozed confidence whilst I, tongue-tied, said almost nothing. And yet the following day, as we were sitting on the hotel veranda with our drinks, I knew I was going to marry him.

Two days after we met, we were in love, and before the end of the holiday Michael had asked my father if he could marry me. It was hardly the most inspiring request for a girl's hand because he actually forgot my name and ended up saying to Dad, "I want to marry... what's her name." I like to think it was due to nerves, rather than how unmemorable I was.

I'd agreed to marry him before I even knew what he did for a living. When I found out he was a hairdresser, I had to laugh. Just like me, Michael came from a line of hairdressers – his grandfather had owned a salon where his mother used to do the shampooing, and he had aunts, uncles, and cousins in the same profession.

When we flew back, Michael's flight got in an hour before ours. He went back to the family flat in Fulham and said to his mum, "I'm getting married, she'll be here in an hour, with her parents and brother".

Celia, faced with the choice of a battle with her beloved only child or bowing to the inevitable, rose wonderfully to the occasion; she immediately put the kettle on and got out the china and a plate of biscuits. At least she was going to meet the girl who'd bowled him over.

When we arrived, Celia was warm and charming. A large woman, she dressed stylishly with immaculate hair (courtesy of Michael) and painted nails. She had the aura of an actress; charismatic and gregarious; the perfect hostess.

Michael's father David was much quieter than his wife. He was a commercial traveller, selling ladies fashions, and he was away from home a lot. Celia had devoted her life to Michael and spoilt him as only a doting mother can. His birth had been 'horrendous', she confided; after a three-day labour she produced a baby who was '27 inches long and hairy as an ape', and announced that her child-bearing days were over. Never again would she go through such an ordeal.

At that first meeting, I suspect both sets of parents were relieved that things weren't worse. Whether we would live to regret our hasty decision, only time would tell.

Duty done, my parents, Paul and I headed back to Darlington.

For the next five months, Michael and I took it in turns to take the train between London and Darlington. Most of our time was spent planning our wedding. Despite advice from everyone around us that we should wait and get to know one another, we were determined to get married as soon as possible, and we booked our wedding for February 25th 1973, six months after we first met.

In those months before we married, I spent a lot of time in the flat in Fulham and I got to know Celia well. I found her a little overwhelming; she talked non-stop while drinking 30 cups of tea and smoking 60 cigarettes a day. She was always kind to me, which was generous of her since I was stealing away the son she worshipped.

Two days before the wedding, I got cold feet. I was about to marry a man who I didn't know very well and move to London to be with him, far from my family. So, I announced to Michael and to my mother that I couldn't go through with it.

My mother drew herself up and turned a steely gaze on me. "Denise," she said, "You are getting married at the weekend. If you want to get divorced after that, then fine, but I'm not telling 200 people that you're not getting married."

By the next day, my jitters had passed.

Back in London after a honeymoon in the Canary Islands. we moved into our new home in South Harrow. The house was in such a state of disrepair that chips of breezeblock fell into the tub whenever I took a bath.

Michael went back to work, managing the Robert Fielding hair salon in Knightsbridge, and I worked at a building society. We scrimped and saved so that we could get our house decorated and repaired. Then came the day I withdrew £200 of our hard-earned money from the bank, to pay the decorator. I left my handbag under my desk at work while I went to the ladies, and when I returned the money was gone. My boss blamed me for leaving my bag unattended, and I sobbed all the way home.

A house that was falling to bits and our stolen savings weren't the only difficulties we faced in our first months of married life; I was out of my depth. At 20 I was a child, while Michael, at 30, was set in his ways. I had no friends in London, and his were all much older than me. I should have taken more notice when Celia said she spoiled Michael, because he had a serious case of 'only-child syndrome'. He expected to be waited on when he came home from work, even though I'd been working too. He was always hungry and wanted supper on the table when he walked in. I wasn't used to having to cook every night, and I racked my brains over what to make. One evening I cooked him a kipper with chips. He ate it and then asked me what was for dinner. I was so furious I went upstairs, packed my bag, told Michael I was going back to Darlington and stormed out of the house.

I got as far as the motorway before deciding that it was too dark to do the long drive, so I turned back and then sat in the car outside the house, too embarrassed to walk back in. I sat there until Michael peered out of the window and saw me, at which point he came out, gave me a hug, and neither of us mentioned it again.

When Michael decided we should have a dinner party, I was determined to show him I could handle the hostess thing perfectly. After studying recipe books for something to impress, I decided to make sticky rice with sweet and sour chicken. So far, so good, except that I overcooked the rice and then dumped it into the sink, clogging the drains. Our guests had come in evening dress, but they all stepped up; the girls to save what rice was left, while the boys took off their jackets to do some plumbing.

Michael's friend Jeff, who had been his best man, disappeared under the sink and undid the u-bend, and a gurgling rush of rice and slimy water poured all over him. I was mortified but Jeff just laughed, and I was forever grateful to him. We saw him often, and we were always keen to hear stories about his adorable six-year-old twin nephews, Jonathan and Neil, who we loved to bits.

I had always resisted hairdressing, but 18 months after we married, bored to bits doing clerical work, I decided I would, after all, train as a hairdresser. Robert Fielding had a school of hairdressing and I applied for a three-month course there. I was accepted, but when I graduated I wasn't offered a job in any of their salons. They took the pick of the bunch, and that clearly didn't include me.

I applied to several other salons but, being shy, I didn't come across well in interviews, and the managers probably felt I would sink in the jungle of salon life. I knew I could be a good hairdresser if someone would let me prove myself, but after several rejections my confidence hit rock bottom.

My parents offered to set us up in our own salon if we returned to Darlington. It was blatant bribery, and it worked. After talking it over, we decided this was an opportunity too good to pass up – so, in spite of Michael's reservations about moving north, we took up the offer and opened Salon 18 in the summer of 1975.

We sold our London house and bought somewhere bigger in Darlington, and life settled into a comfortable pattern; we lived and worked together, and we were back among family and friends. I no longer felt out of my depth. Michael adapted well, he liked life outside London, and business was booming; within a year we had paid my parents back for the cost of the salon.

We became more settled, although we still had some ferocious rows. Michael didn't like me interrupting when he was doing a client's hair and on one occasion, he was so rude to me in front of a client that I left and went home. Frustrated, I had a glass of gin and then another so that by the time he got home I was plastered.

"I deserve an apology," he said. "No way, you should apologise to me," I insisted. We argued until I grabbed a vase of chrysanthemums, intending to throw the contents at him.

Instead, I managed to upend the half-dead flowers and slimy, smelly water, over myself, while Michael roared with laughter.

I loved working as a hairdresser; I got past my shyness by asking clients about themselves, and I was a perfectionist and very creative. Having discouraged me in the beginning, Michael became my greatest advocate and he entered me into the prestigious Wella Vogue national hairdressing competition. The goal was to create a new style; I came up with one I was proud of and made it through the first three rounds of the competition.

The finals took place at the London Hilton. So that only their hair would be distinct, all the models wore an identical dress, designed by Elizabeth Emmanuel who would go on to make Princess Diana's wedding dress three years later.

My hands shook with nerves and it took me longer than anyone else to produce my creation; cornrows across the head from the front to the crown, with delicate sections of hair twisted and threaded with a needle crossways between each row forming an intricate lattice weave, with the hair fanning out at the back of the head, tinted a beautiful shade of honey.

Once we'd finished, the models lined up on stage to be judged. Out in front, a hundred tables were filled with the competitors' friends, family and colleagues, along with representatives from Vogue, Wella and the media.

The results were announced in reverse order, starting with fifth place. Each time someone else's name was called, I felt a surge of disappointment. I was about to pack up my things when the final announcement came; "The winner of the 1978 Wella Vogue hairdressing award is... Denise Jacobs."

Sarah, my model, jumped up and hugged me while the other competitors pushed me towards the stage. As I walked out from the wings, I was blinded by the spotlights. Shading my eyes, I could see a sea of people giving me a standing ovation. It was overwhelming. There was the girl who had been turned down for every hairdressing job I applied for, walking towards celebrity hairdresser John Frieda to collect my award.

Photographs of my style appeared in magazines and newspapers, it was photographed by Norman Parkinson for Vogue, and I toured England giving demonstrations.

Celia was as excited as we were about my win. We visited her and David as often as we could; I had grown deeply fond of her. And then in the summer of 1980, Michael's father phoned to say that Celia was ill. It was pancreatic cancer, and the outlook was not good.

We were due to go on holiday and wanted to cancel, but David told us to go. "If you don't, then Mum will know that something is really wrong," he insisted. We'd been there for a week when he phoned to say we needed to come back.

Celia died ten days later, on July 10th 1980, with David, Michael and me at her side. She was only 68, but her 60-a-day cigarette habit had taken its toll. As she was dying, she held her arms up as though she was looking at something, or someone. Michael thought perhaps she was happy to see her mother, who she had adored.

Michael was 37 when his mother died. Both he and she had expected her to be around for so much longer. She never lived to meet her grandson – but if we thought she was gone from our lives, we couldn't have been more wrong.

1963

12 MINUTES TO MIDNIGHT

Signing of partial test ban treaty between the United States & the Soviet Union

Estimated number of nuclear
warheads worldwide:

32,648

CHAPTER FIVE

MESSAGES

Darlington 1984-1985

"Did you have a boomerang when you were little?"

"What?" Michael looked startled. "Yes. I was fascinated by them. How do you know?"

"Your mother just told me."

"Oh, come off it! I refuse to believe my mother is talking to you."

"She is, though. And she told me about the tortoise you put in the bottom of your grandma's bed."

Michael laughed. "I'd forgotten about that. It did give Grandma a fright."

It was little details like this that gradually convinced Michael that his mother really was communicating with me. She told me about the colour of his school uniform, the brightly coloured socks he loved to wear, and how on Monday nights she would make him egg and chips. She described him taking her to tea at smart department stores on his afternoons off, and how she would phone him, usually when he was in the middle of doing a client's hair, to help her with a crossword clue.

I came to recognise when she wanted to contact me, and to be able to receive her communications effortlessly. It was as though we had a phone between us and I would know when she was on the line.

"How do you do it?" Michael asked.

"By concentrating hard on what your mother wants to say and interpreting the information. It's not easy, but I'm improving," I explained.

While Michael came to accept the truth of what was happening, my parents still insisted that I was deluded and were angry at any mention of me being psychic or of the next dimension. Until, one day, my father's mother and sister turned up.

Dad sometimes dropped in to see me and Dan, and one afternoon we were at the kitchen table having a cup of tea when I realised that someone was making contact. This wasn't Celia, so I was both nervous and excited. My father knew something was happening; he could see my eyes glaze over, my focus and the change in my breathing.

I could feel waist-length, steel-grey hair piled up on my head with old metal hair pins and my body growing to a much larger size. As I looked down, I could see a mid-calf woolly skirt and thick 'American tan' stockings and I could hear my leg dragging on a parquet floor. It was my grandmother, Jane. She had died in 1966, aged 78, when I was 13, so I remembered her well. When my grandfather left her and their seven children, alone and penniless, she suffered a massive stroke; after that she had trouble walking, as one leg dragged. But, despite all the hardship she had endured, she was warm and loving and always delighted to see me.

I told Dad that his mother was with us. He looked unsure whether to believe me or not, but his mother was telling me she was going to give him proof. She told me that my oh-so-serious father had been mischievous as a child. She described the garden of their house; square with grass in the middle and flower beds all around it, and said that one day he went around the entire garden chopping the heads off all the tulips and daffodils until all that was left was a garden full of green stems, with the flower heads scattered around them.

My father was speechless. With tears in his eyes, he nodded. After sending her love to him and telling me that, no matter how difficult things would be for me in the future, I must not listen to anyone other than those from the next dimension, my grandmother left.

I thought it was all over and was about to ask my father if he was alright, when I felt my hair change again – this time to dark hair in the kind of rolls worn in the 1940s, in the WAAF. Someone else was making contact, and I knew immediately that it was my father's sister, Rose.

The hair was the giveaway; as a child I watched mesmerised as she rolled long coils around her finger and somehow pinned them into place. It fascinated me that she could pull her finger out of a roll without it falling apart. Her hair was never cut, and as she aged, she coloured it black and her grey roots would show. No matter how fashions changed, Rose did not move with the times.

"Your sister, Rose, is here too," I told Dad.

Aunt Rose had died at the age of 74, just a few months earlier. She had been sad and lonely for a long time. Her beloved husband Harold had died 20 years earlier of a heart attack, and Rose never got over it. She became a kind of Miss Havisham figure, wearing the same hairstyle and the same wardrobe of clothes that she'd worn when Harold had been alive, and keeping her house just as it was.

Once her two sons had left home, Rose seldom saw any friends, and despite living in the same road as Dad and their brother, Jack, she hardly ever had contact with them. Mum didn't like any of Dad's family (and he didn't like hers either), and Dad had no interest in anyone other than Mum and us three children.

One morning Rose knocked on their door and asked if she could come in for a few minutes, but Dad said, sorry, he had no time and closed the door. Hours later Rose died. She suffered from an enlarged thyroid gland that it affected her ability to swallow. The doctor had warned her only to eat soft foods and never to touch anything with bones in it, but that evening she deliberately ate a lamb chop. A splinter lodged in her throat and she choked to death.

Rose told me that she had been very depressed. I hadn't known this, but my father had. He had ignored his sister's worsening depression and had turned her away when she came to him for help, and he had never told anyone about her visit to him that last day.

After Rose had gone, Dad was silent for a while. "I know she came to me for help," he said. "And I didn't give it to her."

It wasn't until he was dying, almost 30 years later, that we spoke of it again.

"What happened in your life that you would change?" I asked him "Never making time for anyone," he said. "I never invited Rose into the house when she came to me for help.

I wasn't even busy and if I'd given her just two minutes of my time, she might not have died that evening. If only I had taken time to listen to other people's problems and worries, and helped them. I've seen you do that all your life, and I'd like to have done the same."

After the evidence from his mother and sister, Dad accepted that I really did have the ability to communicate with those in the next dimension, and he found this comforting. Mum never did accept it, perhaps because it reminded her of her own mortality and she was petrified of anything connected with death. If I mentioned anything to do with being psychic, she would storm out of the room, slamming the door behind her. But it was enough for me that Dad believed in me. I said a silent thank you to Jane and Rose for that.

While Dad had needed proof, Terry needed careers advice. He often dropped in for a chat and a coffee and one day, early in 1985, he told me that he was fed up with hairdressing and wanted a change but had no idea what he could do that would give him a decent income.

I wanted to help, so I concentrated hard, and a few minutes later the messages began to flow. "I see you getting an offer... that will change your life... When it comes you will recognise it and will have to accept it. I see you travelling a LOT... flying to America and back. You are going to be tired, but you will love it."

Terry laughed. "Thanks Sis, but that's hard to believe. What could I do that would involve travel?"

A few weeks later he told me he'd dropped in to see Dad's brother, our Uncle Bill. He was an interesting man; in 1938 he'd opened a successful factory in London, making small precision components for the British government during

WW2. In the late 70s, when London property prices became exorbitant, he had moved his factory to Newton Aycliffe, outside Darlington, renting space in his younger brother Jack's munitions factory. Our father had moved to work with Bill and Jack – which is how we all ended up in Darlington.

Uncle Bill, who was 80, told Terry that he was getting too old, and he'd decided to close the factory if he couldn't find a buyer. Suddenly Terry saw what a golden opportunity this was and realised what my messages from Celia had been about. He offered to buy Uncle Bill's business; he would run the sales and administration side, and Uncle Bill could still run the technical and manufacturing side.

It was a win-win solution, and it changed Terry's life. He left hairdressing and started running the components factory – a move that involved a lot of travel, which he loved.

Dad, who like Uncle Bill had been an engineer all his life, joined Terry in helping to run the factory's day-to-day operations. One of the first things he planned to produce were bespoke metal cases to house the video players in the boots of the taxis. He explained that due to the complication of tooling up, this might be a little expensive.

"Don't worry one bit, I'll only charge you cost price," he said to Michael and me with a confident grin. "I'll sort it out for you as cheaply as possible."

It wasn't long before one hundred metal cases were delivered at a cost of £110 each. This was far more than I had thought they would cost, but he was adamant this was the cost price.

"If the cases are going to cost this much, we'll need to raise more funds. It never ends," I said to Michael, with a heavy sigh.

As I sat there worrying about what to do next, Celia turned up chuckling.

"What's so funny?" I asked her.

"For goodness sakes Denise, your Dad is ripping you off. It's a swindle," she exclaimed. I could feel the sensation of Celia's belly laugh; no doubt she enjoyed catching her son's father-in-law red-handed. "They were repurposed leftovers from a previous order, fully paid for by the Post Office."

"That little rascal!" I said, before going to tell Michael the story.

"The so-and-so!" Michael said, aghast.

The following day I went to see Dad at the factory. I found him doing paperwork in his office with Terry and his secretary also sat at the far corner of the room.

"Um, Dad, you know you said you would charge us only the cost price of the cases...?"

"Yes," he replied, opening a filing cabinet.

"Well, Celia told me the cost to you was ...er...nothing. Something about their origin being the Post Office?"

Terry and his secretary looked up, mouths open. The drawer closed and there was an embarrassed and awkward silence followed by my father gurgling, as he always did when he didn't know what to do or say next. His cheeks flushed bright red as he spluttered, "Er...Celia is right ... I'll alter the bill. Obviously, the bookkeeper made a mistake". The bill for the metal boxes was absolved and none of us mentioned the 'bookkeeper's' mistake again.

While Terry's new engineering career took off, our Videocab venture was doing the opposite.

The location of the monitor was proving to be a major problem, and work came to a standstill. No matter how we tried, no-one could get it to fit; it began to look as though Michael's idea was stillborn. Until Celia came to the rescue again, and showed me very clearly, a pair of hands pushing the monitor into a hole behind the cab's bulkhead above the window between driver and passenger.

As I explained this to the team, I pointed to the area in question. "There will be a square hole already in place." Everyone laughed, as if to say 'don't be ridiculous', but they got to work and when the padded bulkhead came off, a square hole in the metal was revealed. There was a collective gasp. There it was – the exact hole that we needed, and we had nothing to do but fit the screen into it. No-one ever forgot that moment – it was astonishing.

Now all we had to do was find a monitor to fit the hole. Michael visited several famous companies, but none of them made a mini TV set that would fit the space we had. He telephoned me from a phone box, to say, glumly, that it was all over, but I told him not to give up. "I saw one in my head," I told him. "So, I know you'll find one that fits."

As I was talking, he noticed a sign on a nearby building that said JVC. "I'll try them," he said. "But this is my last attempt, Denise. After that I'm coming home and to hell with your messages. I'm hot, I'm sweaty, and I can't be doing with it anymore!" He rang off and walked into the offices of JVC, where he was immediately shown a monitor that was a perfect fit.

JVC introduced us to Tyne Video Ltd (TVL) in Newcastle and the following month we met Bob Bowden, managing director of TVL to ask if they could order the video monitors direct from JVC and fit them in the taxis. Given the level of technical expertise involved, Bob was dubious about helping us, when I suddenly heard from Celia. What she said was so bizarre that I was hesitant about saying anything, but the message was so strong that eventually I had to.

"Why do I see your father eating six hard-boiled eggs on Monday nights?" I asked Bob.

In complete shock he said, "That is absolutely true! My father did it for years". That was the day I learned that no matter how crazy the message appeared to be, I had to pass it on. After that message, Bob trusted us enough to help.

Meanwhile, Terry offered to let us use his factory space and the know-how of his technical guys to get the motherboard to work. The motherboard was vital; it would bring it all together, playing the videos on the screens in the cabs. But no matter what we tried, it failed and kept bursting into flames.

It had been going on for weeks and the technical team, including Terry, Michael, Paul, Dad, Uncle Bill, and the factory technicians all stood around the workbench where the motherboard sat, scratching their heads in frustration and arguing over why it wouldn't work.

Realising that Celia had joined us, I concentrated intently.

"It isn't working because the X and Y are reversed," she explained.

Despite not understanding what this meant, I tried to tell the technical gang.

"The X and Y are the wrong way round," I squeaked, conscious of my position as the only person in the room with no engineering experience. It was no surprise when my words fell on deaf ears. This was still an era where a woman's place in a factory was limited either to the canteen or to secretarial duties.

I raised my hand to speak, but still no one took any notice.

Eventually I plucked up the courage to say it again, louder this time. "Um, excuse me. The X and Y thingies are reversed." There was silence as all eyes rotated in my direction. A minute later, Bill exclaimed, "Of course! That's it!"

It made sense to Uncle Bill because it turned out that X and Y was an old-fashioned way of describing the problem; only someone of his age would have understood. He explained that the motherboard schematic may have been reversed, which could cause them to short and catch fire. "I'll need to go back and check," he said.

Later that morning he announced that there was indeed an error; the manufacturers had reversed the polarity, so they would all have to be rebuilt.

We had the monitors and the location and now the motherboard was working. The video equipment was housed in the boot. It had sound and on/off switches on the back seat and advertising interspersed with points of public interest.

The business was coming to life. There was just one problem – we'd used most of our savings, and we needed significant investment if the project was to succeed. We'd looked at every option but got nowhere.

One evening I felt Celia making contact. I paused, concentrating hard, and heard her say, "Don't worry, you will meet a short dark man in a square building. He will be standing on a balcony looking down at you, and he will give you the money you need." I turned to Michael and told him what I'd heard. "And guess what," I added. "I didn't have to close my eyes to get the message. That's never happened before." I was thrilled. Michael was less impressed by my eyes-open reception than he was by the contents of the message.

Dad dabbled in shares, and he'd bought some from a

company which he thought might be interested in investing in our project. He telephoned their office and set up a meeting with the directors.

As we pulled up outside their London office in our prototype taxi, I noticed that it was a distinctly square building. We met two directors who were impressed and said they were prepared to float the company on the third tier of the stock exchange. As we were leaving their office, we turned to say goodbye and saw one of them – who happened to be a short, dark man – standing on the balcony, looking down at us, exactly as Celia had described.

Celia's predictions had brought us to this point, but why were we getting help from her? What had we done to deserve it? I felt as though it was all too good to be true – there had to be a reason. Every instinct told me that what was happening to us was not as straightforward as it appeared to be.

I was right. It was just a couple of months after this that I was in the kitchen feeding Dan, and saw the terrible mushroom cloud and the appalling images of dead and dying people that I would never forget. That was when Celia told me nuclear war would change all our lives unless it could be prevented.

That afternoon, as I sat in my kitchen, still in shock, Dad arrived. "I was on my way home from work," he said, "and for some reason I felt I had to come and see you". When he saw my stricken face, he stopped and stood looking at me for a long, thoughtful moment. By some incredible instinct, he just *knew*.

"You've seen something horrifying," he said. "You've just seen World War Three, haven't you?"

"Yes," I said, in tears. Then it all came tumbling out. "The world was on fire, Dad. I saw men, women and children screaming and writhing in unbearable agony, but nobody could help them because they were dying. Innocent people vanished into thin air and the bodies of those left behind were broken, swollen, paper-thin skin hanging from them, burnt to ash, blood oozing from their ears and eye sockets.

"There's going to be a nuclear winter that will last for years. No food, no water, no medical care – just death. How can mankind cause such pain to fellow human beings?"

"Is there anything that can stop it happening?" Dad asked.

"Yes. Peace-loving people can stop it happening if they know it's coming. I am being asked to tell them, but I have no idea how."

"It's a tall order," he said, "stopping nuclear war. But if that's what she's saying and you're the one to do it, well, you'll find a way. And I'll give you all the help I can."

His words comforted me.

Michael was more matter-of-fact about it when I told him.

"I can't for the life of me see the connection between Videocab and nuclear war," he said. "And as for stopping the war, how do you intend to do that? You haven't got a hope in hell," he added cheerfully.

He had a point.

1968

7 MINUTES TO MIDNIGHT

France & China acquire & test nuclear weapons

Estimated number of nuclear
warheads worldwide:

39,443

CHAPTER SIX

A CLOSE SHAVE

London and Denham Village 1985-1987

"Well, this is it. Crunch time."

Michael and I stood on the pavement, dressed in our best business suits and feeling ridiculously nervous. We were about to discover whether the company we'd shed blood, sweat and tears to create actually had legs. Our shares were being floated on the stock exchange. The question was – would anyone want to buy them?

It was a mild September morning in 1985 and we were standing outside the offices of our investors in Mayfair, an area that oozed wealth and privilege. As we went up the marble staircase to the magnificent boardroom with its glass chandeliers, impressive stone fireplace and thick carpets, I smiled to myself. It was a far cry from our jeans and t-shirts days of hairdressing.

Our accountants had put together a three-year business plan showing the viability of the company and its huge potential. If our shares sold, then it could change our lives. If not, well, it might be the end of our hopes and dreams. The directors drank coffee and smoked as we sat around the vast boardroom table, waiting for the phone call. The atmosphere was tense, and I felt sick with nerves. On the table stood an ice bucket containing a magnum of champagne, and next to it were eight cut glass flutes. "Shame to waste that if it all goes pear-shaped," Michael whispered.

The phone rang and one director picked up as we all watched with bated breath.

"Denise, it's for you," he said, handing me the phone.

It was our solicitor, Anthony Fiducia, asking whether we had any news.

We'd been introduced to Anthony a few months earlier, when we realised that we needed a solicitor specialising in flotations. We'd liked him immediately. Tall, slim, full of personality, charming and highly intelligent, he was approved by Celia while we were in his office. "Your father passed away a few years ago, he was a doctor," I told him. Anthony stopped in his tracks. That's how I knew Anthony was the lawyer Celia wanted, and Anthony learned that I was not a typical client.

"Nothing yet," I told him. "I'll call you as soon as we hear anything."

Ten minutes later the phone rang again. The director picked up the handset and after a brief conversation he replaced it. "Is it all over?" I asked looking at his worried expression.

Slowly, his face creased into a smile. "Heartfelt congratulations! The shares were oversubscribed in two hours; we actually have to give money back," he announced.

"We did it!" I screamed, as the champagne cork popped

and we drank a toast to our successful future.

We'd told all our family and friends to buy shares, hoping they would be able to share our success, but plenty of people we didn't know had bought them too. It was wonderful to think that they believed in our company. We had raised a huge sum, and we hoped it would be enough to expand the project until it was self-financing.

Except that, sadly, things didn't exactly go to plan. After a year of research and development it became clear that there were serious issues and TVL couldn't cope with the technology involved. The electronics they were installing played havoc with the original technology in the cabs. In one taxi, a fire broke out. Whilst out on the road, it was not unusual for the newly fitted alarms to go off, and to make matters worse some taxis were broken into and video recorders stolen, much to the displeasure of our insurance company.

It took us a while to get over the problems but eventually we had 350 Videocabs operating in and around Manchester. The drivers were paid a monthly retainer for carrying the system, and they were paid extra for time off the road every month when cassettes were changed and the equipment serviced.

While all of this was causing us a lot of headaches, the advertising was taking off.

Celia had told me that we would successfully sell the advertising slots and, when we began selling in April 1986, she predicted that we would sell 18 ads that month. We did, and after that each month Celia told me how many we would sell. Each month, she was right.

Despite our success in selling advertising space, by late 1986 we were running out of money. Our advertisers were keen for us to put the screens into London taxis, where the money was to be made, but until we could prove to the London Carriage Office that the electronics were completely reliable, we had to carry on our development where we were. As bills mounted and tempers stretched, we came closer and closer to bankruptcy.

"Don't you think Celia may have this wrong?" Michael asked me as he sat, head in hands, in front of a pile of red bills. "Is having all these bills and running out of money in her Greater Plan? Can you ask her to write to the creditors and tell them it's all going to be fine?" He got up and stomped out of the room.

The following day we had a phone call. One of our biggest shareholders was a man called Parvez Latif, whom until then, we'd never met. After introducing himself and asking several questions about how things were going, he announced that he wanted to help in any way he could, and he invited us to meet him at his Knightsbridge offices.

We met a few days later. Parvez was a suave businessman, immaculately dressed and charming. His company, the Knightsbridge Safe Deposit Company, offered wealthy clients security deposit boxes where they could keep their jewellery, bonds, family heirlooms and other valuables in reinforced vaults deep in the basement. Above these were plush offices.

Parvez offered us our own office space and gave us £10,000 to help keep the company going. Now that we had finally got the equipment working, he was very excited about expanding into London, New York, and into aeroplanes and he promised more investment in the future.

So far, we'd managed our jobs alongside parenting a toddler and put every spare minute into the business.

We couldn't continue, it was exhausting – so after much discussion we took a giant step and sold the salon, put our house on the market and began looking for a home for our exciting new start in London.

Months later, unable to find anything we could afford, we wondered if we'd made a mistake, until Celia directed us to a specific estate agent. We asked if there were any properties that fitted our needs and budget, and the agent said no. At that point I realised that Celia had arrived. As my eyes glazed the estate agent looked at me, clearly wondering why this half-crazed woman was staring at him so intently.

"Really? Here?" Michael whispered furiously. "For goodness' sake, Denise."

But Celia was already giving me the message. "I believe you have an A4 buff envelope on top of a filing cabinet upstairs, containing the spec for a house," I said. "Can we see that one?" He looked surprised, but said he would look.

"What are you doing?" hissed Michael.

"I'm just passing on your mother's instructions," I replied, kissing his cheek.

The estate agent returned with the brown envelope. "I don't know how you knew," he said. "But this one has just come in today, so it hasn't been marketed yet." He handed the details to Michael.

"It looks like just what we want," Michael said.

"Shall I organise a viewing?" the estate agent asked.

"We'll take it," I told him.

"But you haven't seen it yet," he said. "How can you be so sure?"

I could hardly say, "Because Celia is telling me this is the one," so I said, "Well, it sounds just perfect."

Mark House was in Denham Village, just outside London, and with easy access to the motorway to get us to Manchester. The house was beautiful on the outside, with a lovely garden, but inside it was very old-fashioned and in need of some fresh paint. We didn't mind that, though.

Given the nature of the mission I had been set, it seemed ironic that we should buy the house that had belonged to a man who had helped create the atomic bomb. A quirk of fate – or was it? What makes man want to create such a thing? Celia explained that people work on inventions, such as the splitting of the atom (which ultimately led to the manufacture of weapons of mass destruction), without grasping the dire consequences.

We moved into our new home in June 1987. Three weeks after the move, we had our presentation launch at the Business Design Centre in central London. We arranged for the taxis, fitted with TVs and video, to come down in convoy from Manchester and to pick up the advertising agents from their London offices so they could watch the system working en route to the launch, where we had erected a huge marquee in the car park.

Over 100 people came, including representatives from newspapers and leading advertising agencies. At the end of the day we were delighted; everything had gone wonderfully.

One of the several interested parties who came was Frank Jarvis, who Michael had known since before we met. Frank was a successful entrepreneur who had all kinds of business interests. He was always on the lookout for new ways to expand his empire and Videocab ticked all the boxes. After the presentation, he took me and Michael to one side and said, "I love it and want the exclusive rights to assist in taking the company forward, subject to due diligence". Michael was elated to have his friend on board – someone he knew he could trust.

Later, we introduced Parvez to Frank. They got on well, and told us they planned to work with us to ensure the project would succeed. We could hardly believe our luck – not one, but two successful business brains. Frank offered to put a £60,000 loan into the company immediately and to arrange the £2 million investment required to get the London operation up and running. For this we agreed to give him an equal shareholding with us in the company. Parvez was already a shareholder, and he told us that he would also be putting in a large sum of money.

It had taken us years of blood, sweat and tears, shareholder investments and the exhaustion of our personal funds put into research and development to get a reliable and fully operational system working. It was an extraordinary sum of money. At last, it seemed we were home and dry.

Our next step would be to lodge the blueprints with the London Carriage Office and New York Yellow Cabs to get permission to commence work in two of the largest cities in the world.

On Saturday July 12th, 1987, Michael and I decided to go to our office to sort out some paperwork. As we parked opposite the Knightsbridge Safe Deposit Company, I said, "I have a strange feeling. Something doesn't feel right and I can't explain it." We crossed the road to the front doors, but they were locked. A 'closed' sign was in the window, which was puzzling since the offices were open around the clock for clients to access their security boxes.

"That's strange," Michael said. "Let's try the back door." But the back was locked too. We drove home, mystified.

A couple of hours later Michael phoned Parvez's security guard John, who told him, "The place has just been robbed, but I can't talk now as we're swarming with cops."

Horrified, I phoned Parvez to see if he was alright. He was clearly shaken and worried about the situation, and said he had no idea who did it. I promised I would see if I could get any information from Celia, but I got absolutely no response.

On the late news, we learned that the place where we'd had our office for the last few months had been cleaned out in what had been dubbed a "spectacular heist".

The Knightsbridge Safety Deposit robbery was declared one of the largest bank robberies in history and the crime of the century. Over 100 security boxes had been emptied and approximately £60 million-worth of jewellery and other goods had been stolen. The final tally was never known, as the people with the boxes – including royalty, millionaires, celebrities and criminals – didn't always want to declare what had been inside them.

When the Scotland Yard fraud police came to interview us, we couldn't tell them much, since we never had anything to do with the security business. But I soon discovered why Celia hadn't helped, when Parvez was arrested for robbing his own company. We were stunned.

John, the security guard had been completely innocent, but Parvez's girlfriend Pam, the receptionist, had also been sleeping with a notorious Italian criminal, Valerio Viccei. Parvez, a cocaine addict and heavily in debt, had been persuaded by Pam to allow the robbery to go ahead in exchange for a cut.

Viccei got 22 years, and was later extradited to Italy to face other charges. Parvez got 16 years. And Pam? The woman who brought it all together got an 18-month suspended sentence.

Only about £10 million of the stolen goods was returned. The rest simply disappeared.

We were shaken. When Parvez kept promising to invest in our business, he probably meant after he got his share of the proceeds from the robbery. Perhaps we'd had a narrow escape. But we were left with our major shareholder in prison, and no offices to work from. Now, it was all down to Frank.

1972

12 MINUTES TO MIDNIGHT

The United States & the Soviet
Union sign arms treaty

Estimated number of nuclear
warheads worldwide:

41,752

CHAPTER SEVEN

THE POISONOUS TOAD

London 1987

Frank was as horrified as we were to hear that Parvez was going to prison and he had lost his business partner. "I always thought he was a bit slippery," he said, which surprised us. We thanked our lucky stars that we still had Frank wanting to help.

If anything, he seemed keener than ever and a couple of weeks later he invited us for Sunday lunch with his wife Jen at their very glamorous home. After detailed discussions, he offered a further £100,000 as long as we put our investment property up as collateral.

This was a concern. Michael had bought a house before we met. It was rented out, which covered the mortgage, and it was our nest egg for the future. We were reluctant to risk it, but after a long night of discussion we agreed that we had to do it. We couldn't turn back now; we had to protect the shareholders who had put their hard-earned money into the company and their faith in us. So, a few weeks later, with heavy hearts, we went to the bank and arranged to put the house up against Frank's loan.

Frank knew all about Celia's role in things. They had met years earlier. "I remember Celia well," he said. He was thrilled when he heard she was correctly predicting the number of ads we would sell each month.

"How many did Celia predict for July, Denise?"

"15. And 18 for next month," I added, and Frank smiled.

"Extraordinary! I want you to meet my cousin Dominic. I'd like to bring him into the business as my partner. I always like to operate with a partner, and Dominic is someone you can trust.

Dominic managed and controlled six of the 20 licensed casinos in London. We met him over lunch, but despite his charming manner and Frank's enthusiasm, Michael and I didn't take to him.

At the same lunch Frank announced, "I want access to everything, including your assets, liabilities and value. I need the names and contact details of all the advertising agencies you're dealing with, all your financial records, business projections, market research, sales information and bank accounts. And I want the blueprints of the motherboards."

"Right. No problem," Michael replied, writing it all down in his notebook.

"Why do you need them?" I asked. I felt nervous and worried.

"Dominic and I don't want to commit until we know the full position." Frank said. "I'm sure you can understand that. It's a lot of money we are talking about here, don't you agree?"

As we left the club, Frank turned to us. "I want to introduce you both to a financier. Come to my home in the cab tomorrow so that he can see it."

The following day we met Simon Smith; short, full of confidence, and a consummate salesman. After shaking hands, we climbed into the taxi with him and Frank. *Aint No Mountain High Enough* blared out over the DHL advert as Michael started the engine and pulled out of Frank's driveway for a spin around Richmond. Simon was clearly impressed.

"And you say you can roll this out in London, New York and on aeroplanes too, if you can raise the finance?"

"Yep," Frank said. "You think you can raise the funds?"

Simon didn't hesitate. "Yes, subject to me going over the company's projections, I can raise the £2 million required."

Frank's eyes lit up, as did ours. As he got out, Simon handed me his business card. "Contact me any time," he said. "I love this project."

We had set up HQ in our home office in Denham, and the following day Frank sent round two men who began checking every nut and bolt of the company's information; they spent days scanning our files, address books, account details and advertising information, including which agents and agencies had made commitments to advertise.

Meanwhile, Campaign Magazine ran an article about Videocab, saying we were an innovative business to watch.

Soon after, an excited Michael told Frank, "We're close to putting in the application to the London Carriage Office. Once they're happy with the technical details, we'll be able to start installing video screens in 16,000 London black cabs. Then we'll be selling advertising space in blocks of 500 cabs. And after that, New York cabs, and then planes."

"Excellent," Frank smiled. "Let me know when the

application finally goes in. How about lunch? We can discuss how we're going to take things forward."

In the restaurant Frank ordered a carafe of house red and three glasses.

"Cheers. Here's to a successful partnership."

Our smiling companion raised his glass towards us and as he did so I stifled a gasp. Slowly his face was turning a dark poisonous green, covered with black pockmarks. He was beginning to look like a toad, but with bright red laser beams coming from his eyes. It was like the product of some over-imaginative special-effects guru, both terrifying and macabre.

I couldn't believe what I was seeing. As he and Michael talked and laughed, Frank's face remained like a grizzly Halloween mask and I knew that it could only mean one thing – danger. Celia was warning me, in the most vivid way possible, that this man was trouble.

Panic clutched at my insides. What was I going to do? Frank Jarvis had become crucial to our plans and our future. How could I persuade Michael and the board – all of them jubilant about how well things were going – that we had made a terrible mistake letting him in?

"What a great guy Frank is!" Michael said as we drove home. "It's like a breath of fresh air having him on board. It should all run smoothly now, don't you think?" He glanced at me waiting for my response, but my mind was in turmoil. I stared out of the window for a few minutes, waiting for the right words to come.

"He's going to do something bad."

"What are you talking about? He's been a friend for years and I trust him implicitly. Not only that, he's a successful businessman, just what we need."

I described the way Frank had appeared as a toad at lunch. Michael laughed and the more I tried to convince him, the more he couldn't accept that Frank was going to betray us.

"Why on earth would he do anything to harm us?" he insisted. "Honestly, sometimes I wish my mother would keep her nose out of things."

"Except that we wouldn't even have this business without her guidance," I reminded him. "I know it's tough, but we have to get rid of him."

We fought about it all night. But Michael still refused to accept that Frank might turn on us.

Despite this, I knew I had to warn the other board members of what I was convinced was coming. At the board meeting a couple of days later, I told them of the toad message I'd received and my doubts about Frank. I could see their disbelief; a couple glanced at their watches as I spoke, barely hiding their impatience.

When I'd finished, all three board members flatly rejected the idea that Frank might be trouble. "You're a paranoid idiot, Denise," one of them told me deprecatingly. "Frank's solid. We're lucky to have him. We can't turn back now."

I understood how hard it was; Frank had seemed like the company's saviour, willing to step up and invest for the future. After losing Parvez, if we lost Frank too, we were back to square one – something none of us wanted to contemplate.

One of them stood up. "I've had enough of this, Denise. We can't run a company on messages from the dead. It's just not something I can do. And this is the last straw. If you don't want to accept Frank's investment, I refuse to be a board member any longer." He grabbed his raincoat and stalked out of the room.

I was shocked. But he was a City man, used to dealing with cold hard facts, and I could see that my way of doing things might seem a little unorthodox, if not downright bonkers – even though he'd seen how accurate Celia's messages were so far and how they'd helped the company.

There was nothing I could do but wait, and hope that somehow things with Frank would work out. But over the next couple of weeks he began to behave more and more strangely. He invited us over for coffee and, sitting on the expensive sofa, he looked over the top of his coffee cup at me and announced, "Denise, I'm not interested in your prediction of world war and messages of peace, this is a business we're running. I want the Manchester operation closed down immediately."

"What? Why?" I spluttered. This was an enormous shock. Manchester was close to our hearts – it was where we had developed Videocab.

"Because it will leave behind all debts accrued, and we can start with a clean slate," he replied, as if this was an everyday occurrence and not one that would affect hundreds of people's lives.

I stared at him in disbelief. "We can't possibly do that."

We had 350 taxi drivers being paid to carry the video screens, our office, mechanics and salespeople who would lose their jobs, not to mention the 82 shareholders who would lose their shareholding.

"Why the hell not?" he asked, irritated.

Next to me, Michael was equally astonished. "Because not only do we have a lot of people depending on us, but we need Manchester to prove to the advertisers and the authorities in London and New York that it can all run smoothly," he said.

The discussion went on for some time, and eventually

Michael stood up to go. I followed him out the door and then turned back, still feeling confused.

"Frank, we can all achieve everything we want if you work with us. You and the company can make money and I can work for world peace too."

He ignored me. "When are the technical blueprints going to be lodged at the Hackney Carriage Office, Michael? Tomorrow?"

Michael looked at him. "Yes."

Frank nodded, waved to us and walked back into the house.

The following morning Frank asked me for a copy of all the information we had sent to the Carriage Office, including the motherboard blueprints. It was late that evening when he phoned and asked, "Is Michael there?" I could tell by his voice that something was up. I handed Michael the phone, and watched as his face turned ashen.

Frank told him that he and Dominic were going to set up a new company and let Manchester go. "We'll buy the patents out of the old company for £100,000 and start trading as a new entity," he had said.

"You can't do that," Michael replied. "We said no!"

"I can do it, actually," Frank told him, before hanging up.

While Frank couldn't actually close Manchester without our agreement, we knew that he was trying to put pressure on us, making closing Manchester a condition of bringing his money into Videocab. And without his investment, we were grounded.

"Now what?" Michael asked me, slumping onto the bed. "I suppose you think Mum will sort this mess out, because somebody sure needs to."

I didn't know whether to scream at the wall or sob with frustration. I had known that Frank was trouble, but no-one would listen. I had no idea what to do next, but I began to sense that familiar feeling of Celia's presence. Was she going to save the day? Michael watched as my eyes glazed and I began to concentrate.

"There is a lawyer in Bermuda, he works for a firm called Vaucrosson. He will make an investment of £100,000 into the company within five weeks. Contact him and be very careful not to let Frank know his contact details."

With that, Celia left me standing in the bedroom with my hand over my forehead shouting, "Bermuda? I don't know a soul in Bermuda." I flopped onto the bed next to Michael, wondering how in the world I was going to find this saviour.

"Simon Smith!" I heard a voice screaming in my head. I ran downstairs and found his business card. With shaky hands, I dialled his number, "What am I going to say?" I asked myself.

"Hello?"

"Hi Simon, it's Denise. I know this sounds a little odd, but do you know someone in Bermuda who's a lawyer at a firm called Vaucrosson?"

"Yes, I do. He's top of my list of potential investors for new companies. His name is Julian Hall."

There was a long silent beat as the penny gradually dropped for both of us.

"Denise, how do you know about this lawyer?"

"Umm... It's complicated," I said. "But could I have his contact number? And could you keep this confidential between us?"

"I understand. Let me call him first and tell him about you, then you can phone him."

Thanking him, I hung up, silently blessing Celia.

Once Simon gave me the go-ahead, I rang Julian Hall. "Hello," I started. "This is probably the strangest call you've ever had. My name is Denise Jacobs and, um... I'm able to communicate with the next world. I've been told to contact you by my late mother-in-law; she said you are the person she wants to help me."

Julian didn't miss a beat. "Tell me how I can help," he replied. I told him all about the company, and he said he found the concept fascinating. "Fax me all the information you have on your project and if it all stacks up, I'll discuss it with a colleague who's looking for an innovative company to invest in and get straight back to you."

I whooped for joy. "It worked," I told Michael, barely believing it. "I found him, and he is interested. We might have a new investor. And that will mean we can keep Manchester going."

Michael and I felt hopeful. We believed that if fresh funds were injected, Frank would relent on wanting to close Manchester. Later that night, Julian sent a fax; "I'm very impressed with your project, Denise. I can see it working brilliantly in the US, and what a wonderful idea for aeroplanes. Please send me the contact details of your solicitor and I will get in touch with him immediately."

"Frank will be thrilled," Michael said when I told him.

At a hastily convened meeting Anthony Fiducia contacted Julian Hall via conference phone. Julian Hall confirmed his intent to invest in the company in the exact terms Celia had told me he would. Anthony asked him for £100,000 as a show of intent for the £2 million investment into the company. Julian agreed, and confirmed that his client was going to put the money into the company.

At the same time, we heard that a separate deal was being set up by Simon Smith with a Greek investor, Emanuel. This was great news – two new investors could only be a positive. Once again, I asked Simon to keep it between us and not to mention anything to anyone else.

The following day we held a board meeting and told everyone about Julian and the Greek investor, and they were delighted. That weekend, Anthony went into his office to discuss matters with Julian Hall and draft the documents. Excited, we waited for an update. But when Anthony called, it was with shattering news.

"Julian pulled out," he said. "He told me that he'd had a call from Frank, who warned him in strong terms not to trust you and Michael. Frank told Julian that he was running the company; his words were, 'The Jacobs are not capable of running it'.

"He said he was bankrolling the company and taking it over, and Julian should work with him and not you."

Anthony had tried to salvage things and told Julian, "I have known Denise and Michael for some time, and I trust them implicitly."

Julian had been fair. "I appreciate that, Anthony; to be honest, I don't know who to believe. Let the dust settle and perhaps I'll get involved later on."

"But how did Frank get Julian's details?" I said.

On Monday morning the phone rang. It was Anthony. "Frank contacted the other investor, and told him the same thing – you aren't to be trusted."

Celia had told me that Frank's greed had no bounds, and here was the proof – he was actively sabotaging anyone else from investing in our company because he wanted it for himself.

We now had two reasons to doubt Frank – he wanted to close Manchester, and he had put two potential investors off. I was worried and I think Michael was too, but he put his doubts to the back of his mind. "Frank knows what he's doing," he said. "Perhaps he warned the investors off because he and Dominic were going to put in enough money to get the London end up and running."

"Something's not right here, can't you see that?"

"Look Denise, I think we convinced him that we absolutely can't close the Manchester operation down. At the next board meeting, when he will be allocated an equal shareholding and accepted as a director and an equal partner, I know he will drive the company forward as successfully as he has done with his other businesses."

Michael was so sure. I decided I had to keep my worries to myself, at least for the moment.

A couple of days later Michael and I, along with the other board members, waited for Frank in Anthony's office. "Now we can get everything sorted," Michael said, as everyone nodded in agreement.

The door opened, and in walked Frank's solicitor. "This shouldn't take long, so let's get started," he said. "I've been instructed by Mr Jarvis to inform you he is pulling out of your company."

"What?" Michael was aghast.

The lawyer ignored him. "He would like the £200,000 he has loaned the company returned to him. You have 14 days from today, failing which a winding-up petition will be issued against your company." There was a loud click as he opened his briefcase, took out a letter and handed it to Anthony. Then he snapped his briefcase shut, stood up and left the room.

As the door closed behind him, it felt as if all the oxygen had been sucked out of the room. Everyone sat motionless and slowly all eyes turned to meet mine. I had been right – Celia had been right – and they knew it. But there was no pleasure in that. It was one of the darkest days of our lives.

1980

7 MINUTES TO MIDNIGHT

Deadlock in talks between the United
States & the Soviet Union

Estimated number of nuclear
warheads worldwide:

55,755

CHAPTER EIGHT

IN SAFE HANDS

Denham Village and London 1988

Two weeks later Frank issued a winding up order, through the Royal Courts of Justice in London.

When Anthony phoned to tell us, I felt sick. "You mean he's actually done it?" I said.

"Yep, he's dragging you through the courts for the money he put in when you gave your house as collateral." Since he had the technological blueprints and all the company information, he was almost there; he was desperate to be rid of us so that he could get his hands on the company and run it with Dominic. "Come into my office this afternoon and we'll discuss how to deal with it," Anthony said.

I looked in the mirror. I was pale and tired. "Why did Celia allow this to happen? What's the point?" I asked myself.

"Keep going, Denise. It will all be alright," I heard Celia say. But how? We couldn't find £200,000 and even if we could, we no longer had any money to keep the company going.

"Denise, I owe you an apology." Anthony hugged me as we arrived at his office. "You said Frank couldn't be trusted, and you were right."

"We're not quitting," I said. "Celia says we mustn't. It will be alright, although right now, I can't see how."

"We need to talk about the next stage," Anthony said. "Frank has issued his writ, and you need to make a defence which has to be delivered to his lawyer as soon as possible. I know the perfect person to deal with this, but," he said, looking at me square in the eyes, "Denise – promise me you won't mention you're psychic. Not a squeak, okay?" I nodded. "Good, then let's go."

The chambers of barrister Charles Purle were Dickensian and steeped in history, with dark wooden floorboards and legal tomes lining the walls. In Charles' office, files were stacked on the floor, with more piled on his desk.

Charles rose. "Welcome to my lair. What can I do for you?" Anthony introduced us, and Charles read the issuing papers. "Hmmm... yes... I can see from the plaintiff's writ that he wants to dispose of you two and throw you to the lions. Well, we can't have that, can we?" He pressed his intercom and shouted, "Clive, we'll have tea for four and lots of chocolate biscuits, please."

Charles turned out to be an absolute legend who merged his deep knowledge of the law with brilliant financial judgement and an understanding of human frailty. A charming man with a twinkle in his eye, he was remarkably astute, and for the next three hours we went over everything that had happened.

At around 6.30pm, I felt my solar plexus start churning with its usual tricks. What was I going to do? I didn't want to upset Anthony, but the message was for Charles and I felt compelled to pass it on. The more I tried to stifle it, the more impossible it became.

"Um, Charles, you're going to see Swan Lake tonight, so perhaps we should carry on tomorrow?" Anthony and Michael glared at me, aghast, as I blurted, "And you're going to become a High Court judge too".

"I don't know if you're right about me becoming a judge," Charles smiled, "but I can help you with the first part". He reached into his inside pocket and pulled out two tickets for Swan Lake. "I'm awfully impressed with you, my dear," he said. "Do you know, I am handling a case in which I must prove whether someone is a real clairvoyant or a fraudster. I can certainly see you are the real thing." As Anthony's and Michael's jaws hit the floor, Charles summoned his clerk. "Can you cancel my attendance? I think this is going to be a long night."

At 3.30am, feeling exhausted and very hungry, we put the outline of our defence through Frank's lawyer's door. We had spent 12 hours piecing together the strongest defence we could.

Jarvis vs Jacobs came to court on June 30th 1988. Michael and I sat behind Charles in the courtroom. My stomach was in knots, and my palms were sweaty with nerves. A few feet away Frank sat behind his legal team, his smug expression indicating his certainty that it was only a matter of hours before he would force us into bankruptcy and lay his hands on our company.

The tension was palpable.

Thankfully, the judge was unequivocal. Frank's wicked attempt to take us over was dismissed and we got our company back – and Frank had to pay all the court costs. He walked furiously away from court, his tail between his legs.

Michael and I hugged one another, and then, in tears, I hugged Charles. It had been a horrible ordeal, but now we could move forward.

It hurt badly that someone we believed to be a good friend had betrayed us, shown contempt for us and selfishly tried to ruin us. But it hurt even more that the company we had worked so hard to create and build had almost been lost.

Simon Smith phoned the following day and congratulated me on winning the case. "How did Frank know how to contact Julian in Bermuda and Emanuel in Greece?" I asked. After a moment's silence, he answered. "I had no idea he was going to do the dirty on you. He asked me to keep him in touch with everything that went on with you, and I just did as he asked."

So now we knew. Simon had been a double agent, keeping Frank informed all the way through. Our attempts at finding alternative investors had never stood a chance.

From now on, we agreed, we would only become involved with blue chip, bona fide, triple-A rated companies. But how would we find one willing to invest in us?

I was in bed when I heard Celia's voice. "Denise, you must contact Julian Hall and meet him." Her instruction was so emphatic that it woke me with a jolt. How could I persuade him to meet? He had dropped out after Frank's intervention, and probably didn't trust me.

As I dressed Daniel for nursery, I was frowning intently. "What's wrong, Mummy?" Dan asked.

"Nothing, Pumpkin. Just wondering how to contact someone, that's all."

"Why don't you phone them?" he asked.

And that's exactly what I did. Julian took my call, happy to talk to me. I told him Frank had lost his case and explained that Celia still wanted Julian's involvement. "Alright. I'm visiting London soon and we'll meet up," he said. I wondered whether he would keep his word.

A few weeks later, Simon Smith phoned. "I feel bad about Frank, so I'd like to make it up to you. Are you still looking for business finance?"

"Yes," I replied.

"I've found a company I can highly recommend. If you look in today's Sunday Times Business to Business section, there's an advert for project finance. I've already dealt with them. I know you want a triple-A company, and they are tied to the Legal & General Assurance Society."

We bought the paper and leafed through to the business section, and sure enough, there was the advert. We phoned and spoke to a man named Kel Cooper, who introduced himself as a financial adviser and appointed representative for Legal & General. At last, the bona fide financial institution we had been hoping for.

A few days later we met Kel at the office of his employer, Romford Financial Services. Outside and in, there were Legal & General posters and paraphernalia displayed everywhere. He handed us his business card, which bore the Legal & General logo, the words 'Appointed Representative' and the acronym LAUTRO (Life Assurance and Unit Trust Regulatory Organisation). We gave him a fully documented history of our company, and Kel assured us he could raise the £2 million we needed for the company, but that we would need to take out Legal & General pensions and insurances for all our staff. "I'll get things started and get back to you soon," he said.

A week later Simon Smith and Julian Hall came to dinner; Julian brought a friend with him, Nick Montgomery. Julian was friendly and relaxed, and he introduced Nick to us as an accountant. Reserved, cautious and thoughtful with a great sense of humour, I liked him immediately. He specialised in accounting, planning and database management, and through Julian he had learned to deal effectively with legal matters too.

Both Julian and Nick were impressed with the project. We told them about Kel Cooper, and Julian said, "Go with Legal & General to start with, they're a huge company. I'll bring in my investor later when you're ready to start fitting cabs in New York and begin the in-flight entertainment in aeroplanes. That's when this idea of yours is going to fly."

It was a strange moment when I looked at Nick and heard Celia's voice, "Tell Nick how you saw Frank as a toad and tell him that you are helping us to call for peace, to stop World War Three." I waited to make sure Celia had nothing further to say, then I repeated her words. Nick didn't bat an eyelid. "I've had a feeling I'd like to put the world to rights too," he said. "And you were right about Frank-the-toad. Simon told me what happened there. Appalling man."

When Nick phoned to thank me for dinner the next day, another insistent voice began to speak. Abruptly, I interrupted. "Nick, you had a brother. He passed away many years ago, his name is Neil." I was aware that I was saying something with enormous emotional significance, but I just had to say it.

Nick was silent. I'd changed the conversation from social chitchat to perhaps the darkest moment any person might have experienced. Neil had died young; the circumstances were unknown to me, but it was clear that Neil was concerned about Nick.

"He's telling me how you love to run. I can see you running for miles along country lanes and your brother always runs with you." Nick explained he had felt so alone after Neil, who was a couple of years older, had died in a tragic accident at the age of 15. The loneliness was re-enforced by being in a boarding school and having to continue with the same routines and the same people, when nothing was the same anymore. He hid his emotions and his grief not just from others, but from himself.

Despite being there when Neil died, he couldn't feel the emotions related to Neil's departure or understand why they were apparently not there. He felt there was a void in place of the sadness and loss he should have felt. And yet these same emotions caused him inexplicable bouts of crying and overwhelming anxiety.

Nick didn't want sympathy. Music helped him to manage those emotions; singing substituted for crying. When he went running, he was on his own, and that was the time he imagined he was with Neil.

"Neil says your office is filled with things you've collected from your childhood as well as a lot of guitars," I said. "You used to play with a wind-up yellow submarine in the bath."

In a voice strained with emotion, Nick whispered, "Yes, it was my favourite toy. No-one else knows about the submarine. I never told a soul."

"Your brother wants you to know he's always with you, he'll never leave you and he sends his love." After that all I could hear was the gentle sound of Nick's sobs.

As was so often the case, I didn't know why I had been given this information to pass to Nick. I simply had to trust that it was all part of a much bigger plan.

Kel Cooper arranged to introduce us to his financiers, Graham Alexander and John Butler, whose company was called SPP (Guernsey) Limited. We met for lunch at the L'Entrecote restaurant in London, where all the diners wore business suits and the room was filled with the low buzz of deals being made.

Kel and Simon were waiting with two others, who were introduced as Graham and John.

"Let's get down to business," Graham said as he finished ordering his food. "I love your project and your achievements so far. You've put in time and effort and your own money to get things off the ground. For you two to have put together and floated your company is highly commendable."

After rounding off their meals with double whiskeys, they offered to fund our project but insisted that their minimum sum would be £6 million – triple the sum we were looking for.

"We only want £2 million," I said.

"Sorry Denise, but we don't do deals smaller than £6 million."

I wasn't happy, but Michael was, thinking that we could put the excess into an interest-bearing account and make some money on it before paying it back.

"Listen, I've been told by the funding bank's solicitor that this financial package is the best thing to hit the City in years," Kel said. The others beamed and nodded in agreement.

"We'll need you to take out an insurance policy to cover the possibility of the loss of the funding," John said.

"How much will this insurance cost us?" I asked.

"£65,000," Kel said.

"We don't have that sort of money! I'm sorry, but we can't

take this forward." Michael and I stood up to leave.

The following day, Kel Cooper phoned. "I understand how you feel, but this is such a great way to raise finance. I can easily arrange the £65,000 deposit for you."

"How?" I asked.

"By re-mortgaging your property."

"And it's safe?" I asked, worried.

"It's 100% safe – I promise," Kel answered.

"Have you known Alexander and Butler for long?" I asked.

"I've done business with them for eight years."

Later, Michael and I talked it over. "Surely a Legal & General representative wouldn't say that if it wasn't true, would he?" I asked Michael.

"Course he wouldn't," he replied. "We're in safe hands now, remember?" He poured a glass of wine for us and we toasted our future.

1981

4 MINUTES TO MIDNIGHT

Soviet Union invades Afghanistan.
Heightened tension between the
United States & the Soviet Union

Estimated number of nuclear
warheads worldwide:

56,371

CHAPTER NINE

ANNABELLE

Denham Village, London and the United States of America 1988-1989

Suddenly, my head was pulled backwards as I felt myself travel back in time. I looked at my hands; they definitely weren't mine, and they weren't Celia's either. They were rough, cracked and sore.

I was wearing a long linen dress and I could feel the eyelets of a corset digging into me. I placed my hands on either side of my waist; it felt tiny. Suddenly, I sat bolt upright and turned my legs to one side, knees and ankles tightly together. What was happening?

We were sitting in our living room with Kel and a man called Carl Fleming, who he introduced as a Legal & General Executive Financial Consultant. The four of us were deep in conversation about the financial package, when I felt the familiar sensation that told me messages were coming through.

Michael glared at me with his 'stop this now' look, but I was already turning to Carl Fleming. "Carl, you live in a very old house in the middle of the country, don't you?" Three pairs of eyes swivelled in my direction. "It's surrounded by a beautiful garden. In the summer it's full of butterflies. In early spring the lawn is covered in snowdrops."

Carl nodded, as Michael and a baffled Kel looked on.

"Your house is an ancient property and at one time it was small, and animals used to live downstairs to keep the place warm so the heat would rise for the people living upstairs."

Silently they waited for me to go on.

"You have an old fire used many years ago as an oven that had a problem, and the builders were trying to sort it out, but they didn't have the knowledge to get the specialised brickwork back together again."

"That's right," Carl said.

"You won the salesman of the year award six times and this year's prize was a holiday to the destination of your choice. You want to go to the Seychelles, and you and your wife were in bed last night looking at brochures. Apparently, you get very frustrated as the old pulley light switch is on the other side of the bedroom, so you have to get out of bed to turn it off, and on cold winter nights you hate that."

"Who is telling you this, Denise?" Carl asked.

I listened for the reply. "My name is Annabelle Towers," she said in a soft, warm voice. "Annabelle still lives in your house with you as she loves it there," I told Carl, passing the messages as I received them from her. "She worked there for years. Every week, she baked bread in the old beehive oven inside the inglenook fireplace and taught the local village children. You've sometimes heard the voices of children singing, haven't you?"

Carl nodded. "Yes."

"Annabelle has something that's bothering her. You recently moved your wooden garden bench from the front of the house, where it sat in the evening sun, to the side of the house where it is completely shaded by the trees surrounding the garden. She would like you to move it back. You see, she loves to sit there, watching the butterflies flitting between the bluebells and buttercups in the garden and fields whilst feeling the warmth of the evening sun on her face."

Having got her message across, Annabelle thanked me for my help and went. The room was silent as everyone tried to assimilate what they had just witnessed.

"That was... astonishing," Carl said. "I don't know how you did it, but everything you said was completely true."

I felt a little shaken, wondering why this episode had happened in the middle of a business meeting.

An hour later, the two consultants had set out their financial package in fine detail.

"To sum up," Kel explained, "in the unlikely event your company should fail, the loan needs to be covered by specialist insurance that costs £65,000. It's not a lot in the scheme of things."

"Is that insurance through Legal & General?" I asked.

Kel shook his head, "No, we don't do such specialised insurance. But everything else in the package is a Legal & General financial product. Once you pay the £65,000 the loan will be transferred into your business account within six weeks, and then you can repay the mortgage." Kel and Carl smiled confidently, put their papers back into their briefcases and left.

Afterwards, I felt Celia standing next to me and I felt myself growing taller as if I was going up in the world of her psychic schooling. "What was that about?" I asked her. "Why did Annabelle come to speak to Carl? I don't even know him; he was just here to do the paperwork for Legal & General."

"All will become clear," was Celia's unhelpful answer. "You have improved your skills, but still have a lot more to learn and understand, Denise." Then she left.

The next morning, I noticed Michael scribbling in an exercise book.

"It's my diary," he said. "I'm keeping a record of everything that's going on. It will be something to look back at when the company is flying high."

I peered over his shoulder. "Oh, you're writing about Annabelle and Carl's garden bench!" I raised an eyebrow.

He shrugged, "Ok, I hold my hands up; I was impressed with your performance".

"Thanks. I still wish I knew why it happened," I said.

Later that day Carl Fleming phoned me. "I've dragged the bench back to the sunny side of the house, as Annabelle asked," he said.

"She'll be so happy you did that," I replied. "Now she can sit in the sunshine again."

"You're extraordinary, Denise," Carl laughed. "I'll never forget you. You've given me so much faith that there is a life-after; thank you for that. And I won't forget Annabelle either, given that she's living with us."

A couple of weeks later, Kel called. "Carl has arranged the re-mortgage based on your joint income from the company, and we've put in place a 21-year Legal & General endowment policy, together with a Keyman policy for you both. I'm going to put in place a company pension scheme, too."

"Sounds great," Michael said.

"One final thing. Graham Alexander wants to confirm that you are aware, before they finalise contracts, that you mustn't get any county court judgements against you at any time, or you will lose the lot."

This was puzzling. Why on earth would we get county court judgments against us? We were still anxious about putting our home on the line, and this worried us even more. "Do you feel happy about it?" we asked one another. And the answer was always the same, "It was arranged by Legal & General, so it has to be safe. They're a huge firm; if we don't trust them, then who do we trust?" We told Kel we were ready to go ahead.

"Excellent! Let's get contracts signed and then I'll send Graham Alexander my invoice as soon as everything is finalised."

"What about Carl?"

"Legal & General will pay Carl his commission on the products you purchase from them. Now, how about lunch at L'Entrecote with Alexander and Butler next Thursday to complete everything? See you there at 1pm, and many congratulations."

When we met for the lunch, on December 1st, 1988, Kel, Simon Smith, Graham Alexander and John Butler were all there.

Graham Alexander was buoyant. "Don't talk, eat!" he said. "I've only got an hour before my next meeting."

"What's that?" I asked, pointing to an object on the table.

"A tape recorder," Graham answered. "I like to have a record of everything we say. This is a huge deal and I don't want any misunderstandings to ruin it. Too much is at stake."

"How are things with Legal & General, Kel?" he asked.

"Everything's in order my end," Kel smiled.

Graham cleared his throat. "Excellent. Michael, if you arrange for the £65,000 insurance cover to be paid into my company account as soon as possible we can get you lovely people on your way."

"Yes of course," Michael said. "And just to confirm, the £6 million will be transferred into our business account within six weeks?"

"If not sooner," Kel chipped in.

"You have my word on it, and I'll confirm it in writing," Graham said as he beckoned the waiter over. "A bottle of Dom Perignon, please."

The sommelier brought it over and Graham handed it to us. "Here's wishing you and your shareholders all the luck with your business. Enjoy this when you get home."

We left the restaurant with Simon Smith, who said, "Once everything is finalised, I'll send you my invoice for £160,000, to be paid out of the loan when it arrives." He climbed into a taxi which glided into the traffic as he shouted, "There'll be films to watch in these soon!"

With the details in place, all we had to do was wait for the money to arrive. We enjoyed Christmas and Dan's fifth birthday as we looked forward to being able to repay the mortgage and our creditors, and to moving the business forward.

After six weeks, no money had arrived. We phoned Kel Cooper who said, "Don't worry it's all in hand, it will be with you soon."

Weeks turned into months. What on earth was happening

to our money? We called Kel every week, and he continued to reassure us that there was just a slight 'hold-up'. Letters arrived from Alexander and Butler telling us that there were technical issues which were being resolved, and promising our funds were on the way.

We were frightened and full of doubt, but what could we do? We felt we had no choice but to trust that the money really was coming. But as time passed, we barely had the money to live on, let alone to pay the mortgage we had taken on for 'six weeks.' Everything we had was in the business; we'd spent our savings, the house that was our pension plan had been repossessed, and we had no income. As we became more and more worried, I started to lose weight and Michael began to look drawn and pale.

I asked Celia what was going on. "Be patient," was all she would say, but it was hard to trust this brief reassurance when our lives were in freefall.

My parents had sold their house in Darlington and moved next door to us. Paul was already in London, and Terry was making plans to leave Darlington too, so they had no reason to stay. They were sympathetic and occasionally helped us out financially, for which we were enormously grateful. But taking their money only made us feel worse.

About that time, Michael's father suffered his final heart attack and died instantly. Michael was grief-stricken.

Then Terry came to visit. He and Sandra had divorced, and he was having a tough time. We sat at the kitchen table in a depressed silence. "I don't know what to do for the best," he said. "I'm so lonely."

A few minutes later I knew Celia was with us and, after focusing, I saw him far away from me. "You're going to live in America," I said, surprised. "And I see you flying back and forwards a lot of times."

Terry laughed. "Don't be ridiculous. That's never going to happen!"

A few weeks later he was invited to a wedding in New York. At the wedding he met a woman who, impressed with a cash-carrying case his engineering company had developed, talked to some of her business contacts about it. The responses were positive and next thing Terry knew he had a fistful of orders and he began flying out to Miami each month, delivering the cases. He made a lot of new friends, fell for the lifestyle and the weather, and decided to move there. Hoping that an English hairstylist might do well in the US, he decided return to his previous profession.

He sold his engineering business and took off in late 1989. He found a vacant shop in South Florida and set up a hairdressing salon. For the first few months, business was so quiet that Terry thought it wasn't going to work out; he was living on savings.

He phoned regularly, and one morning his voice sounded strained. "Sis, I think I'm going to have to shut the shop and return home."

His words faded as Celia took over. "Terry, everything will be fine," I told him. "You're going to be alright." A moment later, an image appeared. "Do you know anyone with racehorses? Celia is showing me a racehorse."

"That makes no sense," he said. "There are no racehorses around here."

"Well apparently there are, and you will be getting someone coming into your salon..."

"Got to go, customer," he said, leaving me listening to the

dial tone.

An hour later he rang back. "Sorry, a woman walked in asking me to do her hair. As I was washing it, I asked her what she did, and she said she trained racehorses a few miles away. I really did think the message was nuts, but I should have known better."

I hung up, amazed. I had just learned how to open my mind further to visualise Terry's future, on the other side of the world. I was incredibly proud that I had managed it.

The message gave Terry confidence, and within three months his business was thriving. I missed him, but I was very happy for him.

Paul, Terry and I spoke to each other at least twice a week, and when Terry flew home for a visit we enjoyed a raucous sibling get-together at my house, reminiscing and swapping anecdotes over eggs on toast. Then Paul paused and became serious. "I've been having odd little gaps in my concentration," he said as he toyed with the food on his plate.

"Perhaps you're just tired," Terry suggested.

"I don't know if this means anything, but driving to work the other day, I blanked out and had no memory of how I got to the office. That kind of thing has happened a few times now. Perhaps you're right, it's overwork and stress."

Terry flew back to the States, and a few weeks later Paul came to see me. As I sipped my coffee, he tapped his finger on his knee; always a sign he had something on his mind. "What's wrong?" I asked.

His smile faded. "My memory lapses have been getting worse, Sis, so I had a medical and I got the results this morning." A tear rolled down his cheek as he struggled to speak. "I have a brain tumour, and I need to have surgery as soon as possible. I'm scared. Will I be okay?"

I hugged him and reassured him. But I was devastated. My bright, beautiful little brother, the baby of our family, was desperately ill. He was only 31. How could it be true? As I wept for him, Michael tried to reassure me that all would be well. "They'll cut it out and he'll be fine," he insisted. I longed to believe that was true, but my gut feeling was not good.

"Celia, please tell me Paul will be alright," I cried as I stood under the shower, wishing the water could wash the awful news down the drain. I didn't expect a reply, but this time she answered me. "Paul will be fine," she said. "He's going to help you in the future."

What did that mean? Was Paul going to join our business? That couldn't be right, because our business was in a desperate state and couldn't employ anyone.

"What are you thinking?" I asked Paul a couple of weeks later as he waited to be taken down the to the operating theatre; his face as white as his sheets.

"Do you really think I'll be ok?"

"Celia said you'll be fine, you'll see."

"Really?"

I nodded and squeezed his hand. The operation took what felt like forever, but when he returned to the room, he gave a weak smile. "I'm still here."

The doctors announced that the surgery was a success – they'd removed the entire tumour.

It was wonderful news.

1984

3 MINUTES TO MIDNIGHT

Further intensification of the arms race between the United States & the Soviet Union

Estimated number of nuclear warheads worldwide:

61,174

CHAPTER TEN

PAUL

Denham Village and London 1990-1992

A few weeks later Paul and I were slouched together on the sofa.

"What are you thinking about?" I asked.

"The radiotherapy; I'm scared stiff. I have to be fitted with a helmet that lets them pinpoint the exact area to target. I'm dreading the chemotherapy too. I was awake all night worrying about it. I'm not even sure how I'll get there every day."

"We'll be happy to take you to hospital," I said, squeezing his hand.

Paul smiled. "Thanks Sis, that means a lot."

For the next few months, Michael and I collected Paul and took him to the hospital. Every session was gruelling and exhausting for him, and watching him become paler each day was hard. After each treatment we got him something to eat before taking him home again.

"Does Celia really say that things will be ok for me?" Paul asked me one day. "I wish she would give me a message." I looked at his pale, anxious face.

"Perhaps she will. We'll just have to wait and see."

One afternoon soon after this, I found myself staring at the phone. The more I tried to ignore it, the stronger the urge I felt to pick it up. Then I realised Celia had joined us, and she was telling me to phone Paul. "Why? Is there something wrong with him?" I asked, but she didn't answer, so I dialled Paul's number.

"Hello?"

Unexpectedly, my father answered.

"Dad?"

"Yes?"

"Celia told me to phone."

"Why?"

"I'm not sure... oh, she's telling me that Paul's eating prunes, is that right?"

"He's in the lounge, I'll go and check."

"Tell him Celia says that eating prunes is the right thing and he'll be fine now." I said, laughing at the bizarre message.

He returned a moment later, chuckling. "Celia's right, again! The treatment's caused constipation so he's eating a large bowl of prunes. When I told him what you said, he grinned."

I felt elated. Celia's message had given Paul the bit of faith he so desperately wanted, and I had now learned the sensation to look for when she wanted me to make a phone call.

One bitterly cold December morning a year after the celebratory lunch where we were told we would have the loan within six weeks, I picked up the post from the doormat, praying there would be a letter to say the funds were about to be transferred.

Instead, there were two letters. One from TVL, threatening to sue Videocab for their fee, and a repossession notice from the building society. In a daze, I handed Michael the letters.

"This means we'll get a county court judgement against us, and then they'll never loan us the money," I said.

Michael picked up the phone. "Listen to me, Kel. It's been a year now, and still no bloody funds. What the hell is going on?"

Kel sounded relaxed. "I can assure you everything is progressing, it's just taking longer than anticipated, that's all."

"How much longer? We have no money to live on, we have a child, we're living on supermarket discounted leftovers, we can't afford heating, and now TVL want their money and the building society is repossessing our home."

"OK, I'll phone Graham Alexander for an update and get straight back to you."

Michael paced up and down the kitchen while we waited.

After what seemed like an age the phone rang. Michael grabbed it.

"I've spoken to Graham," Kel said. "He's in Birmingham, but flying to Frankfurt later to get on with the financing. He'll call you in the morning, but he says the deal is signed."

"How can I believe you after so long?" Michael sounded desperate.

"I have no reason to doubt him. These things can occasionally take longer than expected, Mike. Look, I have to run, but I'm sure he will sort things."

Michael hung up and sighed. "Let's hope Kel 's right," he said.

Two tortuous days later, John Butler called. "Graham left for Zurich this morning, as the financier was not available in Frankfurt. He'll be processing the funding as soon as possible, and I'll write to confirm this. You'll be able to use the letter for the court, if necessary."

True to his word, he wrote confirming that the funding was on its way.

Two weeks later we found ourselves in the county court as the building society tried to evict us. After reading John Butler's letter, the judge gave us a two-month deferment.

We were relieved. John Butler was a solicitor. Surely he wouldn't send such a letter to court unless it was true?

I still had no idea why we were being put through such a painful financial ordeal. All Celia said was, "Be patient, think of the children and keep learning."

I did think of the children, every single day. I would close my eyes and see the images of the nuclear explosion and the bodies of babies and children being burned. Those images made me want to weep every time I relived them. I knew that somehow what was happening to us was part of the greater scheme in which I had to try to stop a nuclear war. But how did it all tie up? I had no idea. All I could do was have faith that somehow it would all make sense in the end.

That faith wore very thin as we were hauled back to court by the building society several more times. Each time we were able to produce a sworn affidavit from John Butler and documentation from the guarantors and lenders to show that our loan was agreed and on the way, and the judge would give us another deferment. But this couldn't go on indefinitely. We were living on a tightrope, borrowing money from my parents to buy food and look after Dan, and consumed with anxiety.

While the wait for our funds was agonising, there was good news from Paul. His treatment had ended and he was doing well. We were thrilled.

One weekend, in July 1991, Paul arrived with a friend. "Hi Sis," he said as he gave me a bear hug. "Meet Philip Bright. He needs a bit of help from you, so I dragged him here." Philip gave Paul a scowl, and I realised he was completely cynical about psychics.

"I don't know if I'll be able to help you, but let's have a cup of tea and see what happens."

He was in luck. As we chatted, my solar plexus let me know I was about to receive an incoming call and I waited for Celia to get going. Paul recognised my expression, but Philip looked from me to Paul, clearly wondering what was going on.

I realised that it wasn't Celia coming through, but a complete stranger and, to my surprise, I immediately started to receive information about Philip.

I described Philip's wife, home, and the nature of his domestic issues to a tee.

Philip looked startled and then asked, "Did Paul tell you what has been going on at home, why I'm here, why I need some advice, anything at all about me?"

"No," Paul and I said together; Philip wasn't at all convinced.

I felt myself moving forwards in time. "Your boss will be made redundant, but you are OK." I edged forward a little further. "In six months, you'll be happy, and in two years you will be happier than ever."

Philip was sceptical, so he kept testing me, wanting more information, and each time I was able to give him details that only he would know and understand.

"Who's telling you this?" Philip demanded.

I had no idea. I waited patiently until I heard a man's voice. "It's your grandfather," I told Philip.

"Can you describe him!" Philip said. I felt myself grow larger and my shoulders pulled back, standing to attention. "He was a big, broad, imposing man who made his presence felt as soon as he entered a room."

"That's him, exactly," he said. "Do you know what he did for a living?"

I looked down and saw a uniform.

"He was in the armed forces," I said. "He had an important job dealing with things under the water." That was as close as I could get, but by this time Philip was close to tears.

"You're one hundred percent right! He was a Commander in the Royal Navy assigned to minesweepers. It was such an unusual job, only he could have told you that."

Now fully convinced, Philip asked what he should do about his domestic situation. His grandfather told him, "Go right now to your parents and tell them everything that's happened to cause Paul to bring you to me. Tell them about your meeting with me and how I am guiding you, and that I said once you talk to them you will know what to do."

"My parents go out every Saturday morning."

"Your grandfather is saying they will be there today."

Philip and Paul left, and Philip later told me that he had gone straight to see his parents who'd decided to stay at home, somehow thinking he would come around. In telling them the story he had been able to see the whole picture and he had known what to do. He got divorced. Six months later he met Deborah and two years after our meeting he married her.

This session was another step forward in my learning. It

was the first time I'd been able to tell what someone's job had been during their lifetime, before they passed on. And I was now able to clearly see into the future. Celia was slowly but surely training me to be able to operate on many levels, which was exciting – and daunting. And every time I achieved the next level, I would ask myself, "How did I do that?"

A few months later, Paul came to tell me that, once again, he had a brain tumour. It was a terrible blow. "I'm terrified. I won't die, will I?" Silently, tears rolled down his cheeks and I felt pain such as I had never experience before. He clasped my hand as I fought back my own tears to be strong for his sake. "You'll be fine, Paul, you'll see," I told him.

In November 1991, Paul underwent another operation. It was a wonderful moment when the specialist told him his operation had been a success. More chemotherapy and radiotherapy followed, and once again Michael and I took him back and forward to his treatment sessions.

Christmas Day came and, against all the odds, it was celebrated with Paul. It was Daniel's 8th birthday, so Paul dressed as PB the Clown and performed his magic tricks once more. I had my precious brother back; the only Christmas present I needed.

Soon after that, two friends, Marilyn and Janet, came round. The three of us spent a lot of time chatting outside the school gates.

I had first met Janet when I noticed her there, waiting for her daughter, and I knew I had to help her. I had walked over and introduced myself.

"This may sound crazy, but your daughter suffers badly from allergies. She needs to stop drinking tap water as the aluminium in it is causing her a lot of problems," I told her.

Janet's jaw dropped.

"Are you okay?" I asked, concerned that I'd said the wrong thing.

"It's just – I took Rachel to the hospital today, and the specialist said not to let her drink tap water as she may be allergic to the chemicals in it. How did you know?"

"It's complicated," I said.

We became good friends, and we shared another mutual friend, Marilyn. When they came to see me Marilyn's father had just died and she was hoping for some kind of message.

"I just want to know he's alright," she said.

I didn't know whether I would be able to help, but as we sat chatting over our tea, I felt that someone was with us, desperate to get my attention. Once I was sure who it was, I turned to Marilyn.

"Your dad is here," I told her.

"How do you know it's him when you've never met him before?" she asked.

"He wants to prove to you that it's him, and that he's alright." I answered. "Have we got a green ink pen?" Michael found one and handed it to me with a sheet of paper. I started writing, and I could feel a man's hand guiding mine as I signed his name; William Stretch. I handed it to Marilyn. "Your father said here's your proof."

Marilyn gasped. "Dad only ever wrote with green ink," she said. "And you don't know my maiden name so how did you know his surname?" She pulled her father's passport out of her handbag and held my version of his signature next to his. They matched perfectly.

It was another first for me, being able to write the signature of someone who had passed and whose name I didn't know. Yet another step in Celia's psychic masterclass.

Meanwhile Paul was visibly deteriorating, and despite our ongoing worry about the business loan, which still hadn't materialised, my focus was now entirely on my little brother. We went to the cinema and Paul stood in the foyer, not knowing what to do. His eyes were vacant, and suddenly I knew he was becoming very ill.

I phoned Terry and sobbed, "Paul is dying." Everything around me was darkening and I wept so much that my throat hurt. "Why can't Celia make him better?"

Paul moved in with our parents and between us we looked after him, watching helplessly as he gradually lost all his motor skills and his eyesight began to fail. He looked pale and thin, and he was very worried about leaving his young children. "I have so many things that I want to tell them," he said.

One warm summer day, Paul and I were sitting on the bench in the garden. He rested his head on my shoulder and I hugged him as he wept.

"What will happen if I die?" he asked.

I blinked away my tears. I had no idea how to answer him. Then I heard Celia's voice and repeated her words. "You'll just fall asleep. You won't know a thing and the next thing you'll know is that you'll be feeling great and in the next dimension ready to start the next phase of your life."

"That sounds good," Paul smiled through his tears. "I hope it's true."

I was with my precious brother every single step of the way as, in the weeks that followed, he became paralysed. There was no more that the doctors could do for him, other than to keep him comfortable.

Terry flew over and before he returned to Florida for work, he said goodbye to Paul, knowing he might not see his little brother again. "Bye-bye, Paul," he said, and kissed him for the last time.

"Bye-bye, Terry," Paul replied, trying to focus on his big brother's face.

Terry went out of the door, sobbing, and called, "See you soon, Paul".

A week later, Paul died, on October 2nd 1992. He was 34.

I had been with him that afternoon, "Sit next to me, Sis," Paul had said tapping the bed with his finger the way he always did. "I want you to have this to remember me by." He pointed to the gold and mother of pearl pill box on the table next to his bed. He told me to open it; inside were a few pound coins.

"It's the last thing I have belonging to me," he said." Whenever you hold it in your hands, think of me and I will come to you."

"I will," I whispered. "I will keep it always."

He raised both his arms, placing his hands behind my neck and somehow found the strength to pull me down so that my cheek lay next to his. "Thank you for being my sister. Thank you for everything you have done for me. Thank you for looking after me. Thank you for everything you have taught me. I love you, Denise."

"I love you too. No-one could have had a better brother." He hugged me for as long as his arms could hold onto me before he let go. I kissed him gently on the forehead and held his hand in both of mine as he fell into a deep sleep, then left him for what was to be the last time.

It was our parents who were standing either side of his

bed when he died in the middle of that night. Afterwards, Dad took Paul's watch off his wrist; I still have it to this day.

Michael and I held one another and wept. I was grief-stricken. My little brother, funny, beautiful Paul, was gone. The world would never be the same again.

1988

6 MINUTES TO MIDNIGHT

Tensions ease between the United States &
the Soviet Union Signing of Intermediate-
Range Nuclear Forces Treaty

Estimated number of nuclear
warheads worldwide:

60,780

CHAPTER ELEVEN

I'LL NEVER LEAVE YOU

Denham Village 1992-1993

The following day I was drying the dishes, and my mind was drifting. And then, suddenly, I could sense something. I stared straight ahead, scared to move.

"Paul," I whispered. "Is that you?"

"I know you can hear me. Concentrate harder."

I took a deep breath and tried to relax.

"Use all your senses, tune in to my vibration. I'll help you," Paul said.

My eyes glazed over, I focused, and the room gradually filled with a pulsating yellow light. Paul told me to look down at my hands. As I did, they took on the shape of his.

"I see your hands, but I can't see you," I said.

"Be patient, as you learn more you will see more."

"How are we connecting? It's like a miracle."

"It's beyond all human comprehension," he replied.

I wanted to cry and laugh at the same time. It truly was a

miracle. Paul had been lost to me, and now he was back. I was filled with emotion, tears running down my cheeks.

"Are you alright?" I asked him.

"Yes," he said. "I am. The moment I left my body behind, I could see again, feel the carpet under my feet, move my arms and legs. I can pass through walls, travel anywhere in the world instantly. After I left my body, I watched Dad take my watch off. I could see our aunt and uncle standing in the hallway as they waited for Mum and Dad.

"I see the past, present and future. It's incredible! So, never visit my grave – I'm not there. I'm here, with you and I promise I will never, ever leave you."

The yellow light began to fade, and Paul said, "I have to go. You don't yet have the ability to keep the link going for longer. Learn to focus harder. Remember that you're here to learn for what is mapped out for you. Nothing can stop that. And I will teach you."

"Paul, don't go... stay a bit longer..."

But he was gone, and I was left with a terrible feeling of loss. There was so much I wanted to ask him. But I knew now that he was with me, he would always be with me, and that was the most wonderful feeling in the world.

Two days after Paul died, my parents came over to our house, numb with sorrow over the loss of their youngest child.

As we talked about Paul, Mum's bottom lip began to tremble. "I want my baby back..." she said, the enormity of her loss engulfing her.

How do you comfort a mother who loses her child? I felt completely helpless. And then I felt myself bathed in Paul's aura and his presence. I wish there were words to explain it, but sometimes there just aren't any. I closed my eyes for a moment as I allowed his love to envelope my entire being for a second time in as many days, and I looked down at my hands; they were his.

How would Mum react if I told her? I so wanted her to know that her son was with us, but her approach had always been very narrow-minded. Might it change now that she had lost Paul?

There was only one way to find out. I took a deep breath. "This is going to be a lot for you to get your head around, Mum, but Paul is here with us, right now."

Mum sat up, rigid, her dark eyes fixed on mine. "What did you just say?" she whispered.

"Paul is saying he wants to give you proof that he is alright."

Mum looked shaken.

"Go on," Dad urged.

"Mum, Paul says he can see everything that is going on," I continued. "He's telling me that this morning Dad went for a walk to collect the newspaper." Dad nodded. "While he was gone, you waited for the washing machine to finish. He says you took the washing out of the machine and found your tights in a complete tangle with the other clothes – such a tangle that in the end you got fed up and had to tear them apart to separate them." Mum's eyes opened wide.

"Is this right Betty?" Dad asked.

"Yes, it is," Mum said. "I threw them in the bin."

"Paul is also saying your engagement ring has broken at the shank and needs fixing."

"Is that true too?" Dad asked. She nodded.

"Goodness," Dad said. "It really is Paul."

Mum said nothing. I watched her expression harden as

her face grew red. She stood up, turned towards me, and with clenched fists banged on her chest and screamed, "Why are you doing this to me? Why are you lying? That wasn't Paul!"

"But it *is* Paul!" I pleaded.

"No! If it was, he'd be giving *me* the messages, not *you*. *You're* just his sister – *I'm* his mother, the first person who held him when he came into the world, not you." Everyone was tense as this scene unfolded.

"How did I know about the tights and your ring?" I said.

"I have no idea, but it wasn't from Paul," she hissed.

I was stunned. I turned to Dad, but he shrugged, as if to say he had no idea what to do. Mum grabbed her bag and stormed out of the house, slamming the door behind her and Dad hurried after her.

I had hoped that Mum and Dad would feel comforted by Paul's message, but for Mum that was clearly not the case. I felt devastated.

My solar plexus was going mad; I felt the intense love from Paul fighting against the distress and anger emanating from our mother, and it made me feel like a pressure cooker about to explode. I broke out in a cold sweat as I ran to the bathroom and vomited.

That night, Michael watched me as I toyed with the food on my plate, unable to eat. "You can't carry on like this, Denise," he said.

I felt very lost. "The mistake I made was believing that someone will accept that the next dimension exists when I give them clear proof." Michael pulled me over to him and kissed my hair. "Not everybody will believe in you, Denise, no matter how much proof you give them," he said. It hurt, but I knew he was right.

Later that night, Paul arrived again. "Life is all about each individual person developing their own colours," he told me. "The way we live our life earns us the colours that form us. The more selfless we are and the more unconditional love we give, the lighter our colour and the higher the vibration. Few achieve pure white, but we all have to work towards it, every single one of us. The more we hate or harm, the darker our colours and the heavier and denser the vibration."

This was what Celia had told me when she showed me the railway carriage.

"What happened to me?" I asked him.

"Instead of closing Mum's negativity off, you went into conflicting energy meltdown. This is one of the things you must learn to deal with."

Perhaps it was just too much for Mum so soon after the loss of her youngest child, but it was also a painful experience for me because I had hoped to comfort her – and so had Paul. Mum never referred to it again, and neither did I. Paul's loss was huge for all of us, and we each grieved in our own way.

Our grief over Paul was compounded by the desperation of our situation. Four years after we were promised the loan, Michael and I were painfully broke and fighting debtors on every front. We clung to Celia's messages to be patient and that all would be well, and Paul came through with the same words.

One day, I was staring miserably at the inside of the almost empty fridge when Michael walked in. "What's for lunch?" he asked.

"Beans on toast – again," I replied.

"That's the fourth time this week!" Michael groaned.

"I'll do the gourmet version, with grated cheese on top,"

I said.

At 3p a can (there was a national supermarket beans war going on at the time, in an attempt to attract more customers), beans were on the menu pretty much every day. We were sick of them.

"Remember years ago, that medium in Darlington told us to carry on no matter how hard things would be?" I asked him, as we ate. "Did she know then just how tough our future was going to be?"

"I don't know, but to be honest, Denise, I'm beginning to waiver... a lot..."

"I don't blame you. What I'm putting you and Dan through is so hard. I wonder every day if I should stop, but how can I? After the horrors I've seen, that we could face in the future, truly I can't. Those terrible images of death and destruction haunt me every day. I swore I'd carry on no matter what, and I must."

"The thing is, how are you going to bring about all this saving-of-the-world?" he asked.

He had a point. I still didn't have a clue. All I knew was that it wouldn't happen until the right time. And until then I had to be patient and keep going.

We fought not to be evicted, not to have our phone, heat and light cut off. We had nothing. We were selling our furniture and anything we could find that would bring in a little money in order to buy food.

Every day we had letters and faxes from the funding bank and their solicitors, confirming that the funds for the business were imminent. We were up to our eyes in official confirmations, which made it so baffling that nothing actually materialised. The brain is a remarkable thing; we believe something because we want to. It would be easy to look back and say what gullible fools we were, but the reassurances we received seemed absolutely genuine. And in addition we had Celia, and now Paul, telling us to be patient, that all would become clear and work out.

Celia told us repeatedly that we must not go to work, she said this was a vital part of the plan. But by late July we didn't know whether we could go on. What if I wasn't hearing the messages from Celia and Paul correctly? Was it possible I was getting them wrong? I needed a second opinion. After much research, I dragged Michael to see a medium who was reportedly very good. Soon after we took our seats in the audience, she pointed to me.

"You are having a very hard time, dear, but no matter what happens you have to keep going as it is all for a special reason, to prove something important for the sake of the children. Take no notice of those who say you are only doing this for attention. Ignorance can be a destructive force."

Those words resonated with me. It was the confirmation we needed. She said exactly what Celia and Paul were saying; how could I risk letting down the children, those living now and those yet to be born? No matter how strange and unconnected the current events in our lives appeared to be, I knew that they would, somehow, lead us to what had to be done for the future of the world.

We couldn't afford to take Dan on holiday. We could barely afford to feed and dress him – although I made a huge effort to get good clothes from charity shops so that he wouldn't feel out of place among his friends. When my parents offered to take him with them to Mallorca, where they had an apartment, we agreed. But it hurt terribly that we couldn't be there. I saw him off at the airport with a huge hug and a big smile and then crumpled onto a seat and sobbed my heart out.

I was forever grateful that Paul would tell me what Daniel was doing when I regularly spoke to Dad over the phone.

"Paul's here, Dad."

"Really? How is he?"

"He's smiling and fine and sends his love."

"Give him my love too."

"I don't need to do that – he can hear you for himself. He says Mum is feeding Daniel rice pudding on the beach right now, is that right?"

"Hang on, I'll go and see." A moment later he was back. "You're right, I mean, Paul is!"

We both laughed at Paul's message and I felt much better, almost as though I could see what Dan was doing, and it was a huge comfort to know that he was happy.

But Michael had reached breaking point. One evening, after sitting in silence, he said, "I've had it, Denise. Let's just stop. I'll get a job; we can start again. I can't live like this any longer, waiting for money that never comes, with our lives on hold. We can't carry on anymore. I can't even afford to put food on the table." He was close to tears.

"It's not your fault, Michael, it's mine," I said.

"How do I know you're not inadvertently deceiving yourself – and us?"

We stared at each other for a long moment as I thought about his words. How was I going to help him? What could I possibly say that would bring him any comfort?

Then, like the cavalry, Celia arrived.

Over the next two hours, as we sat on the sofa in our unheated lounge, wrapped in blankets to keep warm, Celia gave Michael numerous messages. I'd never before been able to communicate with her for so long, and I had to use all my powers of concentration to keep the link going.

She told him of childhood incidents and events that were unknown to me; everything from Michael sucking sugar lumps to him loving Brighton rock in the shape of a walking stick, and biting his nails. She told him about the girlfriend who used to write to him, the football programmes he kept in a cupboard, and the gobbledy-gook language him and his mother used to talk to one another in – and by the end, Michael wept.

It was enough to convince him to go on. How could he stop when Celia was by our side, telling us it would be alright, and everything would eventually make sense? And Paul was doing the same thing. It seemed crazy, but they loved us and we had to trust them.

And then everything changed.

1990

10 MINUTES TO MIDNIGHT

Fall of the Berlin Wall signals the
beginning of the end of the Cold War

Estimated number of nuclear
warheads worldwide:

55,512

CHAPTER TWELVE

DUPED

Denham Village and London 1994 - 1996

"Watch the news," Dad urged. "There's something there you need to see."

He was phoning from the airport; he and Mum were off to Mallorca again and he sounded agitated.

I ran into the kitchen and put on the TV. The 8 o'clock morning news came on and there was a man talking about a new kind of financial crime called advanced fee fraud. He was saying that if anyone had paid money upfront and hadn't received the promised investment, they should contact the Bank of England immediately.

Dread hit the pit of my stomach.

"Do you think that's us?" I asked Michael.

"Possibly," he said, his face ashen. "We need to find out."

I phoned the helpline number that had flashed on the screen and spoke to the man we'd seen on TV. He asked which company we were involved with and when I said SPP Guernsey

Ltd, he said, "Mrs Jacobs, I'm going to put the phone down now. New Scotland Yard Fraud Intelligence will telephone you within the hour. In the meantime, don't use your phone, it may be tapped."

I made tea with shaky hands and we waited. Half an hour later a Fraud Department representative phoned and said the West Midlands Fraud Squad would be coming to see us.

"You must carry on your contact with Alexander and Butler as if nothing has happened. If you don't, you could be in a lot of danger."

Danger? As I hung up, an icy chill swept over me.

Acting as if everything is normal when you know it isn't and you are terrified is not easy, but somehow, we managed it.

48 hours later two detectives were sitting with us in the lounge, asking numerous questions about the deal we had made. "We've been tracking and monitoring these guys for some time now," they said. "They've been committing fraud on a massive scale and they've been dealing in guns and drugs. They were involved with the Colombian drug lord Pablo Escobar, who died in a shootout last December."

"I remember that," Michael said. "It was all over the news. He was a monster who ruined thousands of lives. You mean Alexander and Butler were linked to him?"

"It looks that way."

They explained that borrowers were offered highly attractive deals and encouraged to take out endowment mortgages to cover fees for loans which then simply failed to materialise. We had been duped on a massive scale and a number of other people were in the same position as us. One poor soul had committed suicide.

"They paid their con men mates to monitor the phone

numbers they gave you. They even had a police officer in their pay."

"What happens next?" I asked.

"Carry on as normal until we make our arrests. We'll be in touch shortly."

After they left, we sat contemplating the sheer greed, deviousness and cruelty that had gone into duping us. It was all so professional. Did Kel Cooper and Simon Smith know about it? Or was it just Alexander and Butler who were the villains?

"Kel and Simon wouldn't get their money, since they were due to be paid from the loan, so I imagine they didn't know," Michael said glumly. "Kel must have been telling a porkie when he said he'd done business with them for eight years."

"We've got nothing," I whispered. "We can't keep our home, we can't get Videocab back up and running, we can't pay back the shareholders, we can't even pay the bills or buy food."

Hope had kept us going and had helped us to endure poverty and humiliation. But now that hope was gone, all that was left were the ruins of our lives.

I simply couldn't get my head around it. Why had Celia and Paul told me to keep going and said repeatedly that everything would be alright when clearly that was so far from the truth? What should we do next? Go to work? Go back to hairdressing? Put it all down to a terrible mistake? How could we have been so naïve and stupid?

At that moment, I knew Paul was with me. As always when he appeared, I felt surrounded by a deep, warm loving sensation that I wished would stay with me forever.

"Be patient, Denise. You still must not get a job no matter

how much pressure is put on you. Everything will become clear. We need your help to convey our message to the people of the world. There's much for you to learn before you can achieve what will be required of you in the future. It won't be easy but remember that I will be with you."

After Paul left, I stood staring into the middle distance, my mind in turmoil. What was it I had to learn, and to achieve? I knew my brother wouldn't mislead me, but if we couldn't work, then how on earth were we going to carry on?

Our only hope was that Legal & General would compensate us so we could pay our debts and re-start our lives. We needed them to get us out of the nightmare they'd got us into by repaying the mortgage we'd taken out, reimbursing our loss of income while we'd waited for the loan and refund our shareholders, who had all lost their money. Surely, given the level of their involvement in the whole thing, they owed it to us to put us back to the position we were in before the scam happened?

We contacted them with our complaint and a few days later a poker-faced Legal & General compliance officer came to see us, looked through our paperwork for an hour and curtly insisted, "Nothing here shows Legal & General were involved in any way. The blame rests entirely with the building society."

"How can it be the building society's fault when it was your financial representatives who involved us in the first place?" Michael said. "We went ahead with the whole thing because it was backed by Legal & General – a blue-chip company. How can you deny it?"

He was unmoved. "I'm afraid you haven't got a leg to stand on here. It's nothing to do with Legal & General. You can always approach the Personal Investment Authority. They regulate financial services, offered to the public." He stood up and headed for the front door.

"Now what?" Michael asked.

"Let's try the PIA then," I replied. "It sounds as though they will help."

Fifteen minutes later Michael put the phone down. "What did they say?" I asked him. "That it isn't in their remit," he said. "Now what?"

"I'll call Carl Fleming. Kel introduced him as Legal & General's executive financial consultant, so perhaps he knows how to sort this out."

But Carl said, "I'm sorry, Denise, I've been told by head office that you're making a complaint and I've been warned in the strongest terms not to talk to you." He hung up and I stared at the receiver, stunned.

"Next move?" Michael said

"We need a solicitor."

Our old friend Charles Purle gave us the name of a solicitor who, when we spoke to him a few days later, explained that in order to take Legal & General to court we needed to find proof that they knew about the financial package they sold us, and that Kel Cooper had their authority to arrange it.

"We don't have the proof or the link to Kel, so that's it. It's all over," Michael said gloomily.

"It's not over," I said. "We will find that proof, there's got to be a way."

"Even if we found it, how do you think we're going to sue when we have no money?" Michael said, helping Dan into his football boots.

"I haven't a clue," I replied.

"You're going to need one hell of a miracle to achieve it."

He and Dan gave me a kiss and left for football.

I spent the next three hours looking through all our files of documents again. "What have I missed?" I muttered. "There has to be something." As always, I found nothing.

"How do I keep going when there's nothing to keep going with?" I yelled at the file, as if I was expecting it to reply.

A moment later, my forefinger began tapping on the table as Paul's always did and then the soft yellow glow appeared, telling me that Paul was there.

"Telephone Carl Fleming," he said.

"Legal & General have instructed him not to speak to us."

"Phone now, Denise!"

Just then the door flew open and in walked the boys.

"We won 2-1, Mum!" Dan was full of excitement as he pointed to his grazed knee.

"Our son drew blood for Denham United," said Michael.

My brain was feeling scrambled as I tried to focus on Dan, Michael and Paul all at once.

"Concentrate on me!" Paul said.

I turned to Michael. "I have to phone Carl Fleming right now."

"What?" Michael said.

"Paul's here," my voice was urgent.

"But you're not allowed to talk to Carl Fleming!"

"I know, but Paul says I must."

Michael looked at my fingers tapping on the table and realised what was going on.

"Oh, ok," he said disappearing into the office. A minute later he returned and handed me Carl Fleming's business card. With a shaky hand, I dialled his number.

"Pick up the phone, please, Carl," I willed.

"Hello?"

"Carl, its Denise Jacobs."

There was a pause. "I can't to talk to you, Denise; I could lose my job if I do. I'm going to put the phone down now."

"Please don't. I understand that you can't talk to me, so just listen. Please!"

Silence. He hadn't hung up. I took a deep breath and followed Paul's prompting.

Paul showed me Carl's house – I could see it as Annabelle had described it to me six years earlier. But this time, I was standing inside his house and Paul was guiding me.

"Carl, you have two staircases in your house. If you go up the right-hand staircase it will lead you up to an attic room. If you open the door, there will be a beam of sunlight shining through the window onto a box on the floor on the other side of the room. In this brown box will be a green file that belongs to us. Please will you send it to me?"

Without saying a word, Carl hung up.

Two days later the postman handed me a brown paper parcel. Inside was a green file and stapled to it was a business card signed by Carl Fleming. This folder of documents must have sat in a box for the six years since we met Carl. Surely it had to contain something that would help us?

As I scanned through, I found a folder with the familiar multi-coloured umbrella Legal & General logo on it. Inside were Carl Fleming's handwritten note of Graham Alexander and John Butler's telephone numbers, and Legal & General internal memos showed that Carl Fleming was going to earn £14,081 commission from Legal & General for the keyman policy and our endowment.

I read it again, as the penny dropped.

If Legal & General knew nothing about SPP, as they had claimed, then why did they know about the keyman policy for the project finance from SPP?

"Oh, my goodness." I was tearful. "Thank you, Carl. Thank you, Annabelle. And thank you, Paul." I put my hand over my eyes, trying to take in what had happened. I knew Paul was standing beside me smiling and nodding with pride that I'd been able to interpret his message and get Carl to send us the file. I knew that the information he'd sent wasn't conclusive on its own, but it was a huge piece of the jigsaw puzzle.

When Michael got home, he read through the document. "Wow!" he said, grinning and raising his coffee mug in the air. "A toast to your brother – thanks Paul."

Armed with the file, we returned to our solicitor.

"Looks as if you may have sufficient evidence to get this off the starting blocks," he said. "Are either of you working?"

"Nope," Michael replied glumly.

"Then I can make an application for Legal Aid funds for a barrister's opinion. If he considers this case has merit, we'll issue proceedings against Legal & General. If this case runs to the end, it will mean hundreds of thousands of pounds in legal fees, but given your financial circumstances, with no income, they will be paid by the State."

At long last, Celia and Paul's insistence that we shouldn't work made sense. We shook our heads in amazement all the way home.

The Legal Aid Board agreed to fund a barrister. He confirmed that we had to prove Kel Cooper had authority from Legal & General to arrange the financial package.

"What happens next?" Michael asked.

"I'll draw up an originating summons stating our

claims of negligence, breach of statutory regulations and misrepresentation," the barrister said.

In November 1994 the writ was issued, claiming that Kel Cooper had acted on behalf of Legal & General and was negligent in advising us to take the £6 million loan and then re-mortgage on our property, and in repeatedly assuring us that the monies would soon be forthcoming.

When Legal & General's defence arrived, they denied everything, saying they had no knowledge of the financial package or loan arrangements.

We knew it had to be a monstrous lie, but could we prove it?

Our barrister told us that the next step would be for battle to commence in court. "That won't be for some time," he said, "the wheels move slowly, I'm afraid".

They did. It finally came to court 18 months after the first writ was served. We arrived early, dressed in our smartest dog-eared outfits, and were shown to seats behind our lawyers. As the courtroom filled, the tension was palpable until, finally, in came the District Judge.

Our barrister put our case across convincingly, but when he sat down Legal & General's barrister responded, saying we had no evidence, paperwork, or proof. He suggested the case be struck out to save costs and prevent wasting the court's time.

We waited for an agonising interval as the judge rubbed his chin thoughtfully, until he said, "The Jacobs' case depends upon a finding of negligent conduct. I do consider there is a case to answer; this matter will be set down for trial at a date to be decided upon between all parties."

The battle was on.

1991

17 MINUTES TO MIDNIGHT

The United States & the Soviet Union
sign arms reduction treaty. The Soviet
Union dissolves & the Cold War ends

Estimated number of nuclear
warheads worldwide:

49,342

CHAPTER THIRTEEN

HOMELESS

Denham Village and London 1996 -1997

"Do you mind if we sit here?"

The man sitting at the café table lowered his newspaper. "No, that's fine."

Michael did a double take. "Dominic, hello. Fancy seeing you here."

We sometimes went to our village quiz nights and we'd met Dominic and his girlfriend Claudia there a few days earlier.

"Oh hi," he said. "Of course, sit down. I've been up all night at a party and I don't feel much like chatting, if you don't mind." He disappeared back behind his newspaper as we sat down and stirred our coffees. As I put my spoon down, the messages began.

"Actually Dominic, that's not true, is it?" I said. "You've been up all night at a board meeting. I've got some information for you."

He lowered the paper again. "How do you know I was at a board meeting? And what information? What are you talking about?"

My eyes had glazed over as the instructions for Dominic began to filter through.

"Better grab a pen and start writing," Michael said. "You're going to want to hear what Denise has to say."

Dominic leaned down and took a biro out of his bag and then grabbed a few serviettes to write on.

"You work for a merchant bank and it is about to go bankrupt," I said.

He nodded.

"You can save the bank, but you need the signatures of shareholders, and you will have to go to Germany to get a signature from someone who has a share of the equity."

"There is no such shareholder," Dominic said.

Once again, I was giving information that the recipient had no knowledge of. But I felt confident.

"Yes, there is," I told him. "Once you have all the signatures you will go to Paris, where you will get out of a taxi and walk into a glass-fronted building. You will go through reception and upstairs to an office where you will sign contracts – with a quill pen – which will save the bank."

Giving Dominic these messages, I realise just how fine-tuned my training was becoming. I could see the bank in France so clearly. And my concentration was so improved that I could give complex messages in the noisiest of places; even a cafe packed with people talking.

Dominic looked as though he didn't know whether to believe me or not, but he thanked me and then, still looking perplexed, he got up and left.

Ten days later, as we were watching television after supper, we had a call from his girlfriend Claudia. She had got our number from mutual friends and she sounded upset.

"Dominic is in hospital in Holland," she said. "He freaked out over those crazy messages you gave him."

"I'm so sorry," I said. "Is he alright?"

"He's in the middle of a nervous breakdown," she said angrily. "And it's your fault."

"What happened?" I tried to keep my voice calm, even though I felt upset.

"Everything you said was right, and Dominic saved the bank," she said. "He went to Germany and to Paris and pulled off the deal. But you knew all that stuff, didn't you? You just pretended it was all coming through some kind of weird messages, right?"

"How could I have known?" I said. "I hadn't set eyes on Dominic before the quiz night and the first time I ever spoke to him was in the cafe."

"Well, my friend Daisy says you're a fraud. You've freaked Dominic out. I don't know how you knew it all, but you must have found out somehow."

She slammed down the phone.

I was badly shaken and at the same time very concerned for Dominic. That call had been another powerful lesson for me in understanding that some people will never accept what I do. They are convinced that I have prior knowledge, or make things up, because they simply can't accept the truth.

There were two lovely post-scripts to this story. First, a few weeks later, Claudia phoned to apologise for being so aggressive. She had freaked out at how accurate my information was when I knew nothing about anything. Not long after her call, Dominic arrived on our doorstep with a Jeroboam of champagne to thank me for what I did. He looked well and he said that everything had happened exactly as I described it – even the signing with the quill pen in Paris.

The bank had been saved, but afterwards he'd had a nervous breakdown because of the stress of the previous few months, and he'd split from Claudia, but now all was well. I was touched that he came to thank me – I kept the bottle as a reminder that it really is worth passing on messages to strangers, even ones with volatile girlfriends.

My faith was restored. I had been reminded to believe in myself no matter what – something I would be glad of as the events of the coming months unfolded.

Weeks later we were back in court again, once again trying to save our home from repossession. The judge looked at us kindly. "The evidence shows the promised financial package was nothing but a fraudulent scam, and I have every sympathy for your difficult circumstances. However, you owe a large sum to the building society, and you cannot expect to live rent free any longer. I will make an order for repossession four weeks hence."

That would mean we had to pack up and leave our house a week before Christmas and Dan's 13th birthday. I looked over at Michael's stricken face. I had put him through all this, and he didn't deserve it – and neither did Dan.

I whispered to our barrister, who then stood and put forward our case for a delay. After much discussion, we were given permission to stay in the house for an additional month, but we had to pay £50 a week.

"We don't even have enough money to pay for food," I pleaded. "Let alone an extra £200." But the decision was non-negotiable and we were given 15 minutes to organise the money.

I thought desperately about who we could ask for help, and the only person I could think of was Terry. I fumbled around for my purse in search of coins for the phone. I didn't have enough.

"How much change do you have on you, Michael?" He emptied his pockets – nothing. I ran to the phone box and dialled 100.

"Operator? Can I make a reverse-charge call to America, please?" Fingers fumbling as I took out my phone book with one hand whilst holding the receiver under my chin, I found Terry's number.

"One moment," the operator said. I looked down at my watch; only two minutes before the judge was to return. Heart in my mouth, I prayed that Terry would answer. "Come on, come on," I muttered. With less than a minute left, I heard the operator say, "You have a phone call from Denise Jacobs in the UK, will you accept the call charges?"

"Yes." My brother's voice brought all my emotions to the fore.

"What's wrong, Sis?" Terry asked.

"I'm in court, we've lost our home and they want to throw us out, but the judge will allow us to stay another month if we can pay them £50 per week. We don't have the money. I'm so sorry to ask you, I hate having to, but please can you help us? I don't know what else to do. It's Daniel's birthday and it's Christmas..." I blathered on, tears streaming down my cheeks.

"Course I will."

"Thank you, Terry. I'm so grateful."

Michael tapped his wristwatch. "I must go, the judge is

waiting. Thank you again. Love you."

We returned to the lawyers. "My brother will pay," I said wiping my face with the back of my hand.

Ten minutes later, it was all over.

We fled the court, desperate to get as far away as possible. At home we did what we always did in a crisis – made a cup of tea and sat at the kitchen table, hoping to come up with a plan.

The council housing department was our first call. Michael's shoulders slumped as he hung up; it was breaking my heart seeing him so distraught.

"No council flats, and the waiting list is years long," he said. "I feel I've let you down. I can't even give you a home."

"Don't say that," I said. "It isn't your fault. You haven't let anyone down – in fact you've stood by me all the way through. It's horrible, but for some reason it's what we have to go through. And we'll survive, we have the important things; our health and each other, and our beautiful son."

I was surprised by my own strength of purpose. Part of me wanted to get under a duvet and stay there. But the wisest part of me knew that this was all part of a plan I didn't yet understand.

Over the next days, we spoke to anyone who might help. Our friend Julie gave us the answer. "Find a place to rent and, because you're on the dole, the rent will be paid for you."

"Really?" we both said, astonished. We hadn't known that.

We learned that the Department of Social Security (UK's benefit office) would pay rent of up to £470 a month, but we couldn't find a house anywhere in our area for that sum. Eventually we found the ideal house for £600 a month, and the landlords, unlike many, accepted DSS tenants. With some reluctance, Dad agreed to pay the difference each month.

We sold everything we could, giving us enough to live on for a few weeks and to pay for Daniel's birthday and Christmas presents.

I noticed a battered old acoustic guitar up for auction, bid £20 for it and won, but would Daniel like it? On his Birthday-Christmas morning he ripped off the paper and beamed. "Wicked! Thanks Mum and Dad." His huge hugs meant everything. As far as he was concerned, it was the best present in the universe.

On the morning of January 17th, Michael handed the keys to the local estate agent who said, "Good luck".

As the estate agent closed and locked our front door, I thought back to the time I stood there, all those years ago, waving Carl Fleming and Kel Cooper off and feeling six-foot tall after Annabelle had given her extraordinary message to Carl about his garden bench. Why is this all happening to us? I wondered.

As we walked through the front door of our new home and looked around, I realised how much our lives had changed. Standing in the small, cold, grey living room, I felt we had lost almost everything and everyone.

1988

9 MINUTES TO MIDNIGHT

India & Pakistan test nuclear
weapons as tensions rise

Estimated number of nuclear
warheads worldwide:

26,095

CHAPTER FOURTEEN

EXTRAORDINARY MESSAGES

Denham Village 1997

"I hope you don't think it's too weird, me getting in touch out of the blue like this. I got your number from my brother and I wondered if you could help me?"

Her name was Liz Longley, and she sounded so distressed that I invited her over.

It turned out that Liz was the sister of Nick Montgomery, the accountant Julian Hall had brought to dinner all those years earlier.

"When Dad died, it hit me very hard," she said. "He had always been my rock. He was the best, the one I could rely on no matter what, and now he's not here anymore I miss him so badly." Tears rolled down her cheeks, and I pushed a box of tissues towards her.

"Since his death, I wake up at night and can't sleep. And recently I became aware of the curtains in my bedroom moving, although the windows were closed. And I kept hearing the name Denise in my head, repeatedly. I remembered my brother had met someone called Denise who was psychic, so I rang and asked him for your number. And here I am."

"I'm not sure I can help you," I said. "I can't always, even when I want to. I have to wait to be contacted from the other side."

Liz looked disappointed. "Oh, I see," she said. But then she peered at me. "Are you alright? You look a little... strange."

I'm sure I did. My solar plexus was in overdrive and I knew my eyes were glazing over and my face had the distant look that Michael had described to me many times. Moments later, I was hearing from a man I knew must be Liz's father.

"Liz, I have your father here," I said. "He was blind in his later life, wasn't he?" Liz nodded. "He wants you to know that he is able to see now. He doesn't want you to worry about him any longer. Oh, he's taking me into your toilet and showing me a new loo seat of dark wood with a chrome handle, and he's telling me that you absolutely hate it."

Liz looked astonished. "No-one knows anything about me hating it. I never told a soul. That's extraordinary. And yes, I absolutely hate it. My husband, Jonathan, bought it and when he fitted it, I couldn't believe how terrible it looked."

"Your father wants you to know that this is the proof he's giving you, so that you know he's fine and he is watching what's going on with you."

"That's incredible!" Liz said, laughing. I laughed too. It was such a silly thing to come out with: a loo seat, of all things!

"It's sometimes the most ordinary examples that those in the next dimension use to prove they're really communicating with us," I said. "Your father told you about the loo seat so that you can have no doubt it's him. Now he's telling me he wants to give you evidence of things you won't know anything about."

I waited a few moments as the images appeared. "Apparently, your mother isn't wearing her engagement ring, and she is not sleeping well, so she has taken to having a brandy before bed to help her sleep."

"I'll ring Mum right now and find out if that's true," Liz said. While I made us a hot drink, she phoned her mother and then turned to me, a grin spread over her face.

"Mum just confirmed she isn't wearing the ring and she has started having a brandy every night. I had absolutely no idea."

Over the next hour, Liz's father told her all kinds of other things she didn't know about and needed to check. This was a remarkable step for me – I had learned to give messages to someone who had no idea whether the information was true or not. The boost this gave me was enormous, it was as though it had been arranged to encourage my belief in my own ability and to keep us going.

I was very aware that some of my friends and relatives had deserted me. Convinced I was making it all up, losing the plot and bringing my family into destitution, they had given up on me, so I really valued the ones who still believed in me. One day, as I tried to organise our small living room so that it looked a bit more cheerful, I got a strong urge to contact an old friend, Sue Rule.

Sue's father had died a year earlier, and her mum had been struggling to come to terms with his passing; she was lost and very lonely without him. So, I invited Sue and her mother, Jean, over for tea.

As soon as they arrived, the messages started.

"Sue, is your father's name Bill?"

"It is." Sue and her mother looked at each other, astonished.

"Are you sure it's Dad?" she asked.

"Yes. He's telling me he was in the police – he's mentioning the neck rash from his stiff work collar," I said.

"Yes, that was true." Sue looked amazed.

He described Sue and her sister as young girls, talking about how Sue was a perfectionist, and her sister was the opposite. "I neglected my two girls and they didn't deserve it. I'm sorry," he said. "I was very aggressive, you know; it was part of the job and it became a habit. I was impatient, and I wish I'd acted differently."

As Sue sat, looking dumbfounded, a feeling of love overwhelmed me and took me totally by surprise. I turned to Jean. Once again Bill's words came tumbling out of my mouth.

"Jean, I know I didn't always show it, but I loved you very much and still do," he said. "You've been crying a lot, looking at old photos and feeling lonely, but we will be together again, I am waiting for you."

I watched Jeans eyes fill with tears and at that moment I saw a tall, grey shape with rounded shoulders outside the window. The figure walked right through the wall, across the lounge and over to Jean. I knew at once that this was Bill. He came towards us, leaned down and kissed Jean on both cheeks before taking her hands in his.

Kneeling before her he said, "Jean, you are the love of my life. No one will ever replace you. I died so quickly that I never had the time to say goodbye to you, and that's what I have come to do now."

He had one more thing to add. "Jean, the papers you are looking for are hidden behind the wardrobe in the bedroom."

A moment later he disappeared.

Jean was overwhelmed and tearful, and soon after Bill left Sue took her home. After they had gone, I sat and thought about what had happened. I felt overwhelmed too – it was the first time I had actually seen the form of someone who was passing messages. And what extraordinary messages they had been.

A little later, Sue phoned. "When we got back, Mum and I went straight into the bedroom. We pulled out the wardrobe and there was the box with all the papers she had been searching for."

Just as Bill had promised Jean in his message to her, they did get together again. I was comforted to hear it when Sue and I sat together over coffee once more, soon after her mother had passed away.

"Remember, I promised I'd wait for your mother," Bill told me to tell Sue. "She's here with me now."

I was now learning that our loved ones continue to care for us after they leave this world. They know what's going on in our lives, and even though they are in another dimension, they are able to help and advise us, if we only trust the messages they are giving us.

"Sue and her sister have fallen out," Bill told me.

Sue nodded. "We have – I've been very upset about it."

Bill was speaking again. "Your mother and I have some answers we want to give her."

"Sue, write this down," I said, grabbing a piece of paper and a pen. As Bill listed his points, Sue scribbled furiously.

By the time I'd finished, Sue's face had turned as white as a sheet. Slowly she opened her handbag, took out a piece of folded paper and handed it to me. On it she had written

ten questions she wanted to ask me. As I read through them, I realised that Bill had answered each one – in exactly the same order. Her father had confirmed what the row was about, and what she needed to do in order to resolve things with her sister.

"I can hardly believe it," Sue said. "Both Dad and Mum knew what I wanted to ask you before I even got the piece of paper out of my bag."

These extraordinary incidents gave me the encouragement I needed to keep going forward with the case. Being able to use new skills convinced me my powers were strengthening, as Celia and Paul had said they would, and that helped me to believe in myself and the messages I was receiving.

"We can't give up," I told Michael. "We just can't. We have to see this through."

We had heard that Graham Alexander and John Butler had been convicted of fraud and jailed for six years. That gave us some comfort. But while their case was over with, ours dragged on. The legal wheels turn slowly, and it was often many months between each stage of the court case.

Our solicitor told us to approach all the witnesses we could to see if they would agree to make statements for court; if they agreed, he would get the statements drafted. And we needed to write our own statements. I promised to go through Michael's diaries and get as much information as I could.

Michael's diaries ran for seven years, from 1988 to 1994. That meant 2,552 days to go through. It slowly dawned on me what a colossal and tortuous task lay ahead. For months the two of us sat in that tiny room, sifting through diary entries, typing them up where necessary and cross-referencing them with the evidence, in the form of letters, minutes and other documents.

Legal files arrived from Legal & General, and I sat at the second-hand desk we had installed in our tiny box room we used as our office and scrutinised every document they sent us. Several times I read, "I refer to the minutes of the meeting dated February 1988," but no matter how often I checked, those minutes weren't there. I requested them, but Legal & General's lawyers denied their existence or said they were irrelevant.

I knew they had to exist, and I suspected that they were very relevant indeed. "Why won't they hand them over?" I wondered. "What are they trying to hide?"

One morning our solicitor rang to tell us that Legal & General had written to the Legal Aid Board claiming our case was without substance and doomed to fail. He'd already warned us that Legal & General were drowning him in unnecessary correspondence and irrelevant questions; a well-known dirty trick to increase our legal costs. Eventually Legal & General's endless paperwork ran our funds down to nothing. At the same time, the Legal Aid Board wrote to tell us our funding had been officially suspended as we couldn't prove our case, and our solicitor said he couldn't represent us any more without funding.

Our solicitor informed Legal & General's lawyers that we would continue as litigants in person. But the thought of doing that was too terrifying to contemplate.

"What are we going to do?" Michael asked.

"I honestly don't know," I replied. I looked up at him. "It looks as though this is the end of the road."

2002

7 MINUTES TO MIDNIGHT

Unsecured & unaccounted for weapons grade nuclear material leads to increase fear of nuclear terrorism

Estimated number of nuclear warheads worldwide:

21,561

CHAPTER FIFTEEN

FIGHTING FOR MY LIFE

Denham Village and Bourne End 1999

"Mrs Jacobs I'm sorry to have to tell you this, but you have a grade three malignant tumour."

"Is that three out of ten?" I asked, hoping the numbers went that way. The surgeon looked me square in the face. "Mrs Jacobs, I'm afraid it's three out of four. Let me put it this way; you have a 50% chance of survival.

My heart hammered in my chest. "But I can't have cancer. I'm in the midst of a court case... and... I have World War Three to stop... and we can't afford my funeral, and, anyway... I don't have time to die... I have too much work to do..." I babbled.

The surgeon ignored my outburst. "Fortunately, it hasn't spread to your organs yet, but you do need surgery urgently. I'll remove half your breast from here to here" – he used his ballpoint pen as if it was a scalpel – "and take some tissue from your back here" – he grabbed what little fat I had on my back – "to rebuild your breast." He smiled. All in a day's work to him, but to me pure horror.

It all happened so fast that I was still in shock as I was being wheeled into the operating theatre, leaving Michael waiting; his face as grey as the winter twilight. It was February 1999, just a few weeks after I had discovered a lump in my breast.

"How can this be happening?" we had asked one another. But it was, and we had to dig deep to cope. I was encouraged by knowing that my mother had gone through breast cancer at the same age as me – in fact, in the same month, on the same side, which seemed extraordinary. She'd survived, so I was hopeful that I would too.

We asked for an adjournment, and the judge agreed. But if I hoped I would be left in peace to recover, I was sadly mistaken. Legal & General's lawyers demanded evidence of my medical prognosis; they even wrote to my oncologist requesting updates on my progress, as if I was faking cancer to get out of the case.

After a few weeks of this, I received a call from my irate surgeon. "Will you please tell Legal & General that my job is saving lives, not writing to lawyers hell-bent on wasting my time demanding updates on your medical progress."

"I'm so sorry," I replied, bursting into tears.

He calmed down. "Don't worry, Mrs Jacobs, I'll handle it."

A moment later, I felt Paul's hand resting on my shoulder and his loving aura surrounding me. I had to force myself to stop sobbing so that I could hear his words.

"You'll get through it, Sis, don't worry. You're not going to join me here yet," he said. "And you have to keep going with the case."

"How can I carry on, Paul? I'm not physically strong

enough. You've picked the wrong person to help you, truly you have," I said wiping away a tear.

"You're the right person. You're in the best hands with this surgeon. Keep going, Denise, have faith. I'll be with you every step of the way."

I was grateful for his reassurance. But how could I keep fighting our claim when I was also fighting for my life?

My surgeon, who also happened to be one of the Queen's surgeons, was brilliant – Paul was right about that. He did such a good job that my breast really didn't look any different once I had recovered.

The chemotherapy was grim. By April my hair was coming out in handfuls. The hair follicles on my scalp felt as if they were opening up and bruised. One afternoon I sat alone on the sofa, a Tesco carrier bag on my lap, pulling my hair out clump by clump until I was bald. I sighed with relief as the pain in my head eased. When Michael and Dan returned home, they took one look at me and went white with shock.

I was constantly sick. The taste of food made me nauseous, I couldn't do much more than lie on the sofa retching. Michael did his best to look after me, and we both did our best to protect 15-year-old Dan from too much worry. He'd already been through a lot over the last few years. Thankfully he had his schoolwork, his Saturday job at Sainsburys, and rehearsing with his band to distract him. Dan was naturally talented, and he'd thrown himself into his music.

One day the front door opened and Terry walked in. He and Michael had planned a surprise visit. I was thrilled.

"How's my dear little sister?" he asked, hugging me.

"I'm doing fine," I said hugging him back.

He stood back and looked at me, and I could see his

anguish at how wretched I looked.

"I've got something for you," he said, unzipping his suitcase and pulling out a package covered in bubble-wrap. "When I heard you had cancer, the thought of you dying too... well... I couldn't deal with it. I wanted to do something to give you the faith to carry on and fight this, so I went to the beach and got to my knees on the sand, looking up to the heavens.

"They say there is a grain of sand for every star in the sky, so maybe Paul's in the jar of sand I've brought. I collected some seashells too. If you hold one next to your ear, perhaps you can hear him."

I cried as I emptied the sand into the pretty mosaic bowl Terry had brought. "Every time you're sad or worried, run your fingers through the sand and think of me and Paul," Terry said.

His beautiful gift lifted my spirits. I did as Terry told me, and every time I felt down or afraid, I let the sand run between my fingers, closed my eyes and thought of his love, and Paul's, and the warmth of the summer sun.

I had Paul's little pill box too, and I would hold it in my hand, just to give me strength.

Terry's next move was to get me to eat. A couple of days after he arrived, he invited us to Mum and Dad's for dinner.

"Lovely," I said, knowing that I probably wouldn't be able to eat anything.

When we arrived, the kitchen worktop was covered with fairy cakes, butterfly cakes and mini apple pies. Terry grinned at me with the same mischievous expression that he often had when we were children.

"These aren't just any fairy cakes. I, er, I went to some lengths to get some..." (he lowered his voice and looked around to make sure Dan couldn't hear) "...hash".

"What?" Had I heard right?

"Yes," he said. "It gives you the munchies. Dad grated the stuff into equal quantities whilst Mum and I sprinkled it into each cake before they went into the oven."

I was speechless. My 75-year-old parents and my brother had been making hash fairy cakes for me.

"Think of it as medicinal," Terry insisted, before I could protest. "And before you ask, I made a couple of normal ones for Michael and Dan."

"I'm not at all sure about this," I said.

Terry frowned. "I know you're worried, so here's what we'll do. I'll divide a cake into four. I'll eat a piece and if I don't fall over or make a fool of myself, then you'll know it's safe to have a quarter yourself."

Reluctantly, I agreed. Terry ate his quarter, and we all stared at him for the next five minutes, waiting for him to start laughing uncontrollably, or doing handstands, or tearing off his clothes. We didn't know whether to be disappointed or relieved when the wildest thing he did was sip his tea.

He passed me my quarter of the little pink cake and I ate it. "Mmm," I said. "That's nice. Having just a little bit feels much easier – I really can't eat very much at all at the moment."

"Have another quarter," Terry urged. "Go as slowly as you like."

Half an hour later, Terry and I had eaten eight cakes each and we were rolling around laughing our heads off, tears running down our cheeks.

"Those are very good cakes," I hiccupped, reaching for another one.

"What's so funny, Mum?" Dan said, coming through to

the kitchen.

"Your Uncle Terry," I said. "He's hilarious."

We went through to have supper, and I still felt famished. On TV there was a documentary in which President Clinton was saying, "I did not have sexual relations with that woman," Each time it was shown I called out, "Oh yes you did," before falling about laughing and then forking another huge pile of food into my mouth.

'Operation Munchies' worked. I had never eaten so much in my life; I must have put on a couple of pounds that night. Terry and I started laughing all over again when he rang the next day and told me that after we left Mum and Dad tucked into the cakes that were left, and the result was Dad chasing Mum around the bedroom.

All too soon, Terry had to return to America. We were both dreading the moment we had to say goodbye; it had become so painful since Paul had left us that neither of us could even say the word goodbye to each other; it brought back too many memories.

At London's Heathrow Airport, we hugged. "Thank you for everything," I said. "Especially Operation Munchies."

"Get better soon, please." Terry said, tears in his eyes. By the time he turned to walk through passport control, we were both sobbing.

Terry's faith in me never waned. But for our parents, it was different. Not long after Terry had left, just after I returned home after another chemotherapy session, drained and desperate for some sleep, Dad phoned. He was angry and told me that he wasn't prepared to help us financially any longer. He'd had enough.

I understood, I really did. My parents had helped us for

a long time and it was hard for them to understand why Michael wasn't working, and why I was persisting with the case when I was so ill. But the timing of this felt terrible.

"Dad, we're so grateful for all you've done for us. Please carry on a little longer. Don't do this to us now, not when I have cancer. You know why I'm doing this. It is for the children in the world and their future, not for us."

I hoped he might change his mind, but a few days later my mother phoned to say the same thing. "Can't you see that you're failing Daniel as a mother by waiting around for all these pointless court cases you will never win?" she said.

That hurt. I slumped on the chair with my elbows on the table, rubbing my bald head with my hands. I was throwing up from the effects of the chemotherapy and consumed with worry. How could we continue? I felt I was sinking into a bottomless pit; if Dad wouldn't help, we couldn't pay the rent in full and we'd lose the house. I felt we had no hope left. I was sick and tired and I wanted it all to end.

I had to clear my head, so we went to Bourne End, a little village in Buckinghamshire, for a walk by the river.

I had always loved it there, especially when the local 'celebrity' George the goose waddled over, hoping for bits of bread. I put some on the tops of my trainers and held out my foot as George snapped it up, but even his comical flapping failed to stop the frustration that was building in me like a pressure cooker.

For the next half hour, I strode up and down the riverbank, trying to think sensibly and weigh things up as George waddled in my footsteps.

"I understand why they want me to stop. I get that." I said, talking to George. "But how can I stop?" I muttered, changing direction. "But if I don't..." I turned upriver again. Eventually, I trudged over to Michael and sat next to him on the bank, "I don't know what to do for the best anymore," I said. Then I looked up to the sky and shouted, "Give me one good reason why I should carry on".

We sat in silence for a few minutes, watching the water flow past. Suddenly I could feel Paul behind me, his hand resting on my shoulder.

"Look up at the sky, Sis," he said, and as I did I felt transported forward in time and there was an explosion so huge I felt the earth vibrate below me. I was terrified as I saw a flash of blinding light and put my hands over my eyes. I could see the bones of my fingers as in the sky an enormous nuclear mushroom formed. I could taste a nauseating mixture of foaming blood and metal, and blood dripped from my eye sockets down my cheeks as I witnessed wind knocking down trees as if they were matchsticks while everything around me was destroyed. Buildings were flattened, and bodies lay with the flesh on their bones burned away. I could hear the screams of children and babies, and in a daze, I looked at their blistered faces – mouths open wide to drink the black rain falling from above.

I knew that in the scenario that had unfolded before me, few people would survive. I was transfixed by it. This was more real and devastating than the vision I had been shown 16 years earlier by Celia.

"What's going on, Denise?" Michael asked, alarmed by my horrified face.

I told him what I'd seen.

"Where's it all going to start?" he asked

"The Middle East. The catalyst will be centred around

Iran."

"You must have that wrong. Don't you mean Iraq? That's where all the problems are right now."

"No. Iran is definitely the catalyst and the build-up to it will begin in 2025. This war will seal the future path for centuries to come because millions will be killed or starve to death, and millions will live in a nuclear winter. No-one will escape the consequences, unless we can make the world and its leaders listen to Paul and Celia's warning."

I had now been given extraordinary new information – I hadn't known before where WW3 would originate, and I hadn't known when.

My mouth felt dry. I was terrified. How could I stop so much death and destruction? Who would listen to me? How could I prove that what I had seen was real? How could I pass this warning to those political leaders with a hunger for absolute power? I knew, with fresh clarity, that I had no choice but to carry on. But how? And how could I convince the world I wasn't lying?

A moment later, I heard Paul's gentle voice reply to my questions. "You will achieve this mission when the time is right. We need your help. Without you, we can't warn of what is to come, or to help humankind to change the future. The young must be given the chance to live their lives, and they must be told the truth."

"What truth?" I asked him.

"The truth is that we exist, and from here we can see the past, the present and the future," he replied.

"How will that be proved?" I asked.

"I will show you how."

"And how do you think the world will take it, even if I can

warn them?" I said. "Won't people think I'm just a nut?"

"The future is in everyone's hands. All we can do is warn them of what is coming. Don't listen to Mum and Dad, listen to me. You must carry on and all will be fine. Terry will help and protect you because he knows you're telling the truth." Before I could ask him about this, Paul switched tack.

"Be careful. Legal & General will try to discredit you and your mental state by saying you believe in spirits from another world who are telling you everything will be alright."

Then he had gone.

I told Michael what he had said.

"Well, they're right about you and the spirits," he said. "But obviously that won't sound good in court. They'll try to make fools of us and call you a nutty eccentric. They'll try to use it to get the case thrown out."

"Yes," I said. "I'm sure that's what they'll be planning." I felt very worried. Things just seemed to keep on getting tougher, and at every turn I wondered how on earth we would succeed. We were David to Legal & General's Goliath, and at the moment we didn't have a slingshot to our name.

2007

5 MINUTES TO MIDNIGHT

North Korea conducts nuclear tests.
Iran's nuclear ambitions

Estimated number of nuclear warheads worldwide:

12,995

CHAPTER SIXTEEN

NIGHTMARES

Denham Village, Uxbridge Library and Bristol 2000-2001

"Denise, it's alright, you're safe."

Slowly my eyes focused on Michael's worried face.

"You had another nightmare, just try to breathe slowly."

I realised that the gasping, whimpering sobs I could hear were my own. My body was drenched in cold sweat and I was trembling violently. I closed my eyes and the horrors of the night returned. The choking black smoke, the flames, the agonised screams, people running in all directions, their skin peeling from their bodies, others clinging to the dead bodies of their children.

It was a nightmare I had increasingly often. The horrors Celia had first shown me on that sunny morning back in 1983 had never left me, and they'd been reinforced by the visions I'd had at Bourne End. The terrible images haunted my waking thoughts and my broken nights. And always there were the questions; what is it I must do? How am I meant to warn the world that this nuclear horror is coming? When is everything that's happening to us going to make sense?

After the nightmare I would lie awake for the rest of the night, restless, scared, and desperate for a way forward.

As I finished chemo, radiotherapy followed. It was exhausting; I felt like a small, bald, hollowed-out version of the woman I had once been.

I was horribly tired, but I couldn't afford to sit around recovering. I needed to get back to the court case, which was due to continue in a few months. I had faith in Paul and Celia, but we still didn't see how we could win without the evidence and without legal aid.

"Okay Paul, what do I do now?" I asked, wondering if he would answer.

Then I felt his presence. "You must go to the library and research litigation and the law around financial institutions and practice."

"What? You want me to study law?" I didn't know whether to laugh or cry. Why couldn't I just have an ordinary, uneventful life with my husband and son? I didn't want to study law or fight a court case. I didn't feel capable of handling such a monumentally insane ask.

Did Paul think I could take on Legal & General without a lawyer? It seemed he did.

"You can take this case on, and I will help you," he said.

The thought of doing it on our own filled me with terror. But I did as I was told, and the following day I dragged Michael off to Uxbridge library and began pulling out books on the law. "There are hundreds of them! Where on earth do we begin?" I said.

Over the weeks that followed, I studied continuously; in the hospital I'd study in the waiting room. At home I'd stir soup with one hand and hold a law book in the other. Everywhere I went, I'd be hunched over legal tomes. To my amazement, I was able to absorb it all very easily. I liked the logic and the order involved with law. "If I'd known I had this ability, I would have studied law years ago and made us rich by representing wealthy clients," I whispered to Michael one day as we sat in the library.

"Shhhh," the librarian hissed at us. Michael rolled his eyes.

I was reading about in the law on Ostensible Authority when I heard Paul's voice. "Research the back issues of *The Times* and *The Sunday Times* on Joe Palmer."

At the microfilm projector I scrolled through the newspaper pages. "Stop now," Paul exclaimed.

The article was headed 'Watchdog chief has "blemished record"', and it was in *The Times* newspaper dated March 17th, 1994:

> *"A Labour MP has attacked as 'extraordinary' the appointment of Joe Palmer as the head of the Personal Investment Authority after Legal & General had been fined record £400,000 inc. costs for 'serious breaches'. Mr Campbell-Savours questioned why Mr Palmer was appointed chairman of the PIA when 'it is he himself who presided over the affairs of the Legal & General throughout the period when the Lautro rulebook was so comprehensively and regularly breached'."*

I printed off a copy.

"Read this," I said to Michael.

"Bloody hell!" Michael said. "The Personal Investment Authority is the body that is supposed to regulate the financial services industry. This looks a lot like a case of poacher turned gamekeeper to me. No wonder when we approached the PIA they didn't want to know about our case."

No wonder indeed. We had approached the PIA when we realised that Legal & General had no intention of compensating us. They had told us they couldn't help. And here we were, learning that the PIA was run by the man who had presided over serious breaches of the rules when he was head of Legal & General.

You couldn't make it up.

The following morning, I felt that warm sensation of love that told me my brother was there. "Is that you, Paul?" I asked.

"Yes," he replied. A wave of emotion took me by surprise, I felt exhausted and weepy.

"I'm so tired, Paul," I whispered. "I have no idea what to do next."

"Telephone a Member of Parliament called Dale Campbell-Savours. He will send you something that will help you."

"He was the one mentioned in the article, wasn't he? I can't phone someone who isn't even my MP," I said.

"You can. Hurry up, phone him now," Paul insisted.

Hesitantly, I picked up the phone and dialled, wondering what on earth I was going to say.

"Houses of Parliament," the receptionist said.

"Dale Campbell-Savours' office, please," I asked nervously.

Would his staff even let me speak to him? Then I heard a voice. "Dale Campbell-Savours."

How had Paul known he would answer the phone at that moment? I was so shaken I stumbled over my words.

"Um, er... my name is Denise Jacobs and I'm stuck in a legal case against Legal & General. We've lost everything, and I think perhaps you can help me."

"Go ahead," he said. He listened without interruption. "This issue is very close to my heart," he said. "I'm going to bike over the Blue Book together with some documents, Denise. Read it all very carefully, and then do everything you can to bring your story out into the open. I want to expose what is going on in the industry, and perhaps you can play a part in this."

I gave him my address and hung up, amazed. How did Paul do that? Did he really know where everyone and everything was? It was incredible.

A couple of hours later a courier arrived with Dale Campbell-Savours' Blue Book; it contained the House of Commons' minutes from various committee meetings in which questions had been asked regarding practices being carried out by the finance industry in Britain.

"It's going to take days and days to read all of it. It's like *War and Peace* with extras."

"Rather you than me," said Michael.

I started reading. On every page there were revelations that supported our case. I spent days recording all of them in our evidence files.

While I worked night and day on the case, I thought a lot about Paul saying that Terry would help us with our housing situation. When Celia appeared, urging me to phone him, I picked up the phone and dialled his number. It was good to hear his voice.

"Terry, it's me," I stuttered.

"What's wrong, Sis?" he asked.

"I don't want to ask you but I have no idea what else to do," I said. "Dad feels he can't help us any longer, we have to leave our rented house and I just don't know where to turn. Paul and Celia said that you would help; I don't know if you can, Terry, but I just wanted to ask you if you might be able to help us pay the extra rent for a while so that we don't end up homeless again."

"Well, it so happens that I just discovered that I have some money I didn't know about in an old account in England. Enough for the deposit on a house. So how about you find a small home and I take out a mortgage? You can pay me back when you can, and there's no pressure or time limit."

"You would really do that for us?"

"'Course I would. I love you. I don't know how you will succeed in what you're doing, but I know you can do this. Just keep listening to Paul and Celia, they will guide you through it."

"You're the most wonderful brother," I said fighting back tears.

"You've done a lot for me too," he said. "Your messages have helped me so many times. You can't put a price on that."

"Thank, you, thank you again, Terry, for everything," I said.

As I hung up, I couldn't believe what had happened. I told Michael and we hugged. We found a little house in nearby Hillingdon; Terry paid the deposit, and the DSS covered the mortgage repayments. We no longer needed any money from my parents, and that was a huge relief.

I was grateful for my parents' help over the years, but they were growing older.

Dad rang me one day, very wound up. "Your mother hasn't been well for a week now. She's like a child, repeating things over and over. If she's not the centre of attention, she gets furious. I don't know what to do," he said.

After that, he phoned me about her behaviour most days, asking me to come round and it was soon very clear that Mum was in the early stages of dementia. It was heart-wrenching seeing her disintegrating before my eyes and returning to a childlike state.

That wasn't our only nightmare.

Almost two years to the day after the first cancer diagnosis, I sat in my surgeon's room, hoping to get the all-clear.

Instead he looked at me, his face grave. "It's bad news, Denise," he said. "I'm sorry to say the X-ray has picked up a tumour in your other breast. I'm making arrangements now to book you in for a biopsy and a scan."

The news hit me like a train.

"What's my prognosis this time?" I asked.

"We'll need to wait for the tests to confirm it, but I would say it's the same as last time, you have a 50% chance of survival. I'll need to operate again, and as before there will be chemotherapy followed by radiotherapy." He looked at my chalk-white face and did his best to be reassuring. "You've done this once before, Denise, you can do it again." Easy to say; I had no idea how I was going to face this second onslaught and emerge still standing.

It was all tougher the second time around. But as Michael said, what choice did I have? It was a question of putting one foot in front of the other and keeping going. I got through the operation and spent a week in hospital recovering. Then came the chemotherapy and another five weeks of radiotherapy.

I was painfully thin and suffering incredible thirst from the chemotherapy. And I couldn't sleep at night, for weeks on end, so I would crawl into bed in the afternoon unable to move a muscle.

As before, Legal & General continued writing to my oncologist for updates, asking when the court proceedings could continue. The pressure from them was relentless, and I felt my resources totally depleted. Would I ever recover? But the human body is a marvellous thing and a few months later there was some much-needed good news. "You're in remission," my oncologist said, and this time he was smiling.

How do you thank someone for saving your life? I flung my arms around his neck and kissed him on the cheek. He smiled awkwardly, pink with embarrassment.

Michael was thrilled, his relief apparent. Dan was ecstatic. For one brief moment, we celebrated what had, at times, seemed impossible. I was clear of cancer.

Then, reality burst my bubble as I realised I needed to get back to work. We were appealing against the withdrawal of our legal aid, and we were due to face the Legal Aid Board.

"We need to convince them, because we desperately need solicitors again," I said to Michael.

A few days later we drove to Bristol where we were shown into a meeting room where three people sat across a table from two empty chairs. "Take a seat," the hatchet-faced woman in the centre indicated.

She looked at us. "Each member present has received a copy of these files from the lawyers for Legal & General. It is quite clear you have no evidence as to their liability in this matter and they claim you are vexatious litigants whose case is doomed to failure. What do you say about these accusations?"

I was talking to three brick walls.

"I see the defendants' case is that you simply took out a re-mortgage in the normal course of business, and that Mr Cooper was not acting as agent for Legal & General in his dealings with you."

"That's not true at all," Michael blurted out in frustration.

I flicked through the files in front of me until I found a copy of Kel 's business card. "Here is Kel Cooper's business card. It clearly states he was tied to Legal & General." I passed it across the table.

The chairman looked at it and handed it back. "You will receive our decision in due course."

As we walked down the stairs and out of the building we were both silent, lost in our own misery. Outside, I noticed the name on the front of the building next door.

"Look whose office is next door to the Legal Aid Board, Michael." I said, pointing up at it. He looked up, shading his eyes from the winter sun.

"Bloody hell. It's Legal & General's firm of solicitors," he replied.

We stared at it, not knowing what to think.

By the time we got home, I was exhausted. The last two years had been gruelling, and my energy levels were still not back to normal. But, despite this, I couldn't sleep. I tossed and turned while watching the yellow of the streetlight cast long shadows over the room.

"You need to get some sleep, Denise." Michael murmured. "Things will seem better in the morning. Would a cuddle help?" He put his arms around me and it did help, but sleep was still elusive. I eventually crashed out as the birds started their morning song.

When I woke and went downstairs Michael was sitting in the kitchen staring out of the window, a letter on the table in front of him.

"Is it more bad news?" I asked.

"Our appeal for legal aid has been turned down. Now what are Paul and my mum going to do?"

I had no words. I was too tired even to think clearly.

Meanwhile the court had given an order for the case, which had been put on hold due to my ill health, be lifted. The case was to be resumed.

But how would we fight it?

2015

3 MINUTES TO MIDNIGHT

Modernisation of nuclear weapons
in the United States & Russia

Estimated number of nuclear
warheads worldwide:

10,161

CHAPTER SEVENTEEN

WE NEED A MIRACLE

The Law Courts, Denham Village, and the British Library 2002

"My Lord, I wish to insert into the Defence that the plaintiffs believed that 'spirits from another world' had told Mrs Jacobs that everything would be alright," stated Mr Odgers, Legal & General's barrister.

Michael and I had exchanged disbelieving looks. Paul had told us this was coming, but it was still a shock to hear it in open court.

The judge looked bemused. "I see," he said. "And how did you learn of this, er, spiritual guidance, Mr Odgers?"

They'd got the information from photocopies of Michael's diaries, and they said they believed it reflected my mental state.

This was the hearing to set the case in motion again and I was representing us for the first time. I was terrified sitting on the front bench, with Michael beside me and the terrier-like

Legal & General lawyers on the opposite bench. So, when the judge asked if I had anything to add, I said I didn't.

Thankfully, he took very little notice of this intervention. He moved on to warn us that, if we couldn't prove that Kel Cooper had authority from Legal & General to act for them, then all our claims would fail and we would be liable for all court costs, which could amount to many hundreds of thousands of pounds.

He gave us six weeks to prepare our witness statements, adding, "There will be no further delay. This case is so old that witnesses may well pass away if we delay any further." He chuckled at his own joke, and then turned to me.

"Mrs Jacobs, I fear you will need a solicitor at worst, and a miracle at best."

We had six weeks in which to prove our case or lose everything.

At home, Michael said, "How can we win? Everything's stacked against us. You're exhausted and as thin as a stick of spaghetti, and I'm worn out. I just wish we'd never started this thing. We could have had a good life, with jobs and a house and a life that wasn't taken over by your damn messages from the other side... and instead we're just chasing moonbeams." He had tears in his eyes.

What could I say? We both realised what a monumental task lay ahead, and the dire consequences if we lost – and not just to us personally. If I couldn't prove my case, then I couldn't prove that Paul and Celia really were giving me messages and that the warning about nuclear war was real.

"I don't have all the answers," I said. "I wish I did. But I trust Paul and Celia. Look at all the incredible things you've witnessed. Remember Philip Bright's grandfather explaining the job he did in the war? Nick Montgomery's yellow submarine? Marilyn's father's signature? How could I have written his signature when I'd never even met him? How could I have known he always used green ink?

"Remember the wonderful Annabelle who continues to enjoy sitting in the sunshine to this very day? And Carl Fleming's two staircases? What about the sun shining onto the green file in Carl Fleming's attic room? And the notes Sue Rule had in her bag? How could I have got those answers in the right order unless her father told me? How did I know he had left his important correspondence in a box behind the wardrobe in the bedroom? Please don't give up on me now, Michael."

He nodded, "You're right, all those things were amazing. But I'm still afraid you might be wrong about this."

"Think of the fact that Celia and Paul insisted I start studying the law, long before we lost the legal aid appeal. They knew what was coming. We have to trust them for this last step. I will never forgive myself for the financial harm I've done to you and Dan," I said. "But now we only have six weeks to go before we give them our witness statements and then that hurdle is over, and we can go on to the final stage. We have to give it our best shot or..."

"We have nothing." Michael interjected. "We will be penniless and homeless and we'll owe hundreds of thousands of pounds in legal costs."

"Yes," I said.

After very little sleep, I went into our tiny office. It was freezing cold because we couldn't afford heating. I pencilled 42 lines on a piece of paper and wrote *Countdown to Court* at the top of the page. Then I stuck it on the wall, took a red pen and struck through the first line. "One day down – 41 to go," I thought.

I continued studying law by day and putting together witness statements all evening, and often half the night. I was so driven that I barely ate, and the more pressure that built up, the less hungry I became. "You can't carry on like this," Michael protested, looking at my weight loss and ashen face.

To make things even worse Legal & General's lawyers piled on the pressure by making spurious requests for information in order to drown us in paperwork and leave us less time to put our case together. Their lists of questions always turned up on Friday afternoons and the questions had to be answered by Monday, entailing a whole weekend of research. It was the two of us against the might of their substantial workforce.

At the British Library where we went daily to gather evidence of the rampant mis-selling within the financial services industry, the photocopying limit they imposed – no more than 10% of any volume – was nowhere near enough, and Michael took to stuffing extra photocopies inside his sweater. Thankfully the security guard never noticed Michael's stomach was bigger when he left than when he arrived, or the rustling noise he made as he went through the exit.

At home, stacks of files and documents were piled from our little office into the hallway and onto each step of the stairs as the evidence piled up. Everything had to be copied three times, collated in date order, numbered, and given a covering sheet marked 'Exhibit 1' through to 'Exhibit 2000' (or more) ready for court.

"What is it I'm not seeing?" I shouted in frustration as I stared at the endless files of documents. I needed a way to see the whole picture – so just as in all TV crime shows, I used Post-it notes, wrote the names of main players and events on individual ones, and stuck them all over one wall, connecting them with ribbon.

I stood back and studied my work of art. "Why can't we prove what they did?"

As I stared at the wall, deep in thought, Dan popped his head around the door. "Coming to watch us play tonight, Mum?" he asked. "I've written this new song. I could do with your support."

Dan, now 18, was writing some beautiful music and the band was starting to get bookings; I longed to go and watch them, and I felt miserable saying no. I sat at the computer, bleary-eyed with exhaustion, until Dan stuck his head round the door again. "I'm off Mum. You sure you don't want to come?"

I shook my head. "See you later, good luck." My boy was growing up and I was missing it. I went into his bedroom and held a piece of unfinished music. The one track he kept saying he couldn't finish without spoiling it.

I'd been told by Paul that there would be a book of my story, and a film, and that Dan's music would be the soundtrack to the film. It all sounded incredible and highly improbable. Whatever the future held though, at that moment, I was missing my son's big moment, and I wept.

I returned to the office to carry on typing, ploughing on like a robot until I heard Michael and Dan return.

"Shame you missed it, Mum. It was wicked!" Dan yelled as they carted everything in.

"I wish I'd been there," I said.

"Perhaps there's just no evidence to find," Michael said.

But there had to be. Didn't there?

"Let's go to bed. We can carry on in the morning."

"I can't, time's running out and there's still so much to do. You may as well get some shuteye, I'll be fine." Michael, clearly worried, kissed me on the head and left for bed.

I switched off our old computer as the sun was rising and crept down the unlit stairs. Suddenly I lost my footing and tumbled down, crashing onto the floor as dozens of files landed on top of me. My coccyx hurt and my elbows were grazed and bleeding from carpet burns. Michael and Dan found me in a heap on the floor, and I groaned with pain as Michael helped me up the stairs and into bed.

"Get some sleep," he ordered as he slid into bed next to me. But sleep was impossible. I had no idea what to do next and felt I was drowning.

When Michael slipped out of bed in the morning, I heard the door shut softly behind him. My body felt bruised and sore and as I turned over, my scuffed elbows chafed against the sheets. My chin began to tremble and then the floodgates opened. "I can't go on anymore," I sobbed into the pillow. "Paul, I'm sorry – I don't have the strength to go on."

Near my bed stood the pretty mosaic bowl containing sand and shells that Terry had brought for me from America when he was worried about my contracting cancer. I got out of bed, put out my hand and let the white sand run between my fingers. Then I picked up a shell and placed it against my ear. I smiled as I heard the Atlantic Ocean lapping on the Florida shores. "Paul," I said, "If you really want me to succeed with this case and to prove that from where you are you can see the past, present and future, you will have to help me now."

A glimmer of yellow light filled the room; I stood still,

afraid to move as I watched it deepen to a golden yellow. Overwhelmed by love, I felt Paul's hand rest gently on my shoulder and I knew his heart ached for my pain. "I'm here to help you, Sis," he whispered. "Go and phone Nick Montgomery, right now."

I stumbled into the office, searched through my address book and found the business card Nick had handed to me 14 years earlier, in September 1988, the night Julian Hall introduced him to us. With shaking hands, I dialled his number.

"Come on, Nick, please answer," I said, worried that he wouldn't want to talk to me.

"Nick Montgomery."

"Hi Nick, it's Denise Jacobs."

"This is a blast from the past, Denise. Hello. How are you?"

"I'm fine. It has been a long time, but I need your help," I said, the clammy palm of my hand sticking to the phone.

"What can I do for you?" Nick asked.

I waited for Paul's instructions and focused on what he was showing me.

"Nick, you have an office at the bottom of your garden, don't you?"

"Yes! How do you know that?" he asked.

"I'm being shown it. Please could you go down there. You will see, in the eaves, there is a buff folder hanging up. In it, there is information relating to our case. Would you send it to me?"

"Denise, I have hundreds of buff folders in my office. And I'm pretty certain I haven't got anything relating to you or your case, but it's been a while, so just to be sure I'll go and see. If I find something, I'll send it on."

"Thank you so much, I really appreciate your help, Nick."

The luminescent yellow haze was still with me. "I'm proud of you, Sis," Paul said. "Keep going."

The thought of him leaving me made my eyes brim with tears once more. "This is so hard," I said as I watched the shimmering colour surrounding me disappear.

In the bathroom I groaned at the haggard face and dark-ringed eyes staring back at me from the mirror.

Nick was so sure he didn't have anything that would help me. Would Paul have guided him to find anything? And if so, how useful would it be?

I waited in an agony of anticipation. Surely there was a folder, there had to be. And it had to contain something to help our case.

Two days later the postman knocked and handed me a parcel. Inside was the buff folder Paul had described. Pulling out the contents on the kitchen table I could see there were numerous documents dated from February 1988 onwards, including a handwritten document, in black ink, headed 'Finance Facility'.

I started to read and very quickly I knew, beyond doubt, that I was looking at the document I had searched for and requested so many times, and that I had been assured did not exist. The missing minutes. This dog-eared, 14-year-old handwritten piece of paper was the evidence we needed to prove our case. The minutes of a meeting confirming the marketing strategy that Legal & General were at such pains to deny.

I grabbed Carl Fleming's green file, the one located when I directed him up to his attic room, with the yellow ray of sunlight shining onto it.

I opened it, put the two files together and the hairs stood up on the back of my neck. "My goodness, the jigsaw is complete!" I shouted.

All I could hear in my head were the judge's words when he said, "Mrs Jacobs, you will need a lawyer at the very least and a miracle at the very most."

We had our miracle.

"Thank you, Paul," I whispered.

2017

2 MINUTES 30 SECONDS TO MIDNIGHT

Renewed threat of arms race between the United States & Russia

Estimated number of nuclear warheads worldwide:

9,435

CHAPTER EIGHTEEN

JACOBS VERSUS GOLIATH

The High Court, London 2002

As we sat on the packed tube train home, a grin spread across my face and I felt giddy with excitement. I handed the documents I was reading to Michael and he shook his head from side to side, his smile broader and broader until eventually he looked at me and we both burst out laughing.

We were reading the Legal & General's witness statements, and the evidence Paul had uncovered made every one of their assertions look ludicrous. It took several minutes before we both looked up and, much to our embarrassment, we realised our laughter had spread throughout the carriage.

Earlier that day, Michael and I had arrived at the Royal Courts of Justice in London's Strand, each of us lugging several plastic carrier bags filled with page after page of our witness statements and exhibits. The building's imposing Victorian Gothic architecture and intimidating atmosphere underlined the gravity of our situation. After waiting in a long queue to get through security, we walked into the Great Central Hall and onwards through myriad corridors lined with centuries-old oil paintings of monarchs and judges. We'd finally arrived flustered outside our designated court to find Legal & General's lawyers already there sharing jokes with each other. They looked fresh and relaxed and with the self-assured hubris you would expect from a team of lawyers awaiting their legally unqualified opponents.

"Here are our witness statements," I had said, handing over the Tesco carrier bags to one of the lawyers, who took them with a grimace of distaste. In return we received a slim black file containing the other side's witness statements.

In the court, the judge, raising his eyebrows at the array of wilting plastic bags piled up around the Legal & General's lawyers, ordered the pre-trial review for ten weeks' time, on September 20th. Both sides were ordered to exchange discovery documents – in other words, all the information relevant to our cases – no less than a week beforehand.

After the laughter in the carriage subsided and we had finished absorbing the weakness of their witness statements, we were convinced Legal & General would throw in the towel.

"Surely it will be over now? How can they possibly win against such strong evidence?" I said.

I hadn't counted on their determination to grind us down. Weak as their case was, they weren't about to give up. They continued to deluge us with lists of questions, usually on Friday afternoons, demanding replies within 48 hours. But we were not going to be beaten into submission – not now that we had come this far. I painstakingly answered every question they sent, and somehow was able to remember the date and content of every single letter, fax and document we had.

"Impressive," Michael said, as I reeled off yet another set of facts in answer to yet another question.

After weeks of intense work, we had just two days to go. Dan, Michael and I dragged our evidence to the local print shop where it became a frantic race against time to get everything copied, all of us sweating liberally under the pressure.

I was exhausted and collating the documents back at home. I got to number 1,521, and suddenly had no idea what came next. I stared like a zombie at the next page.

"Mum? Are you okay?" Dan asked, putting his hands on my shoulders. "When was the last time you ate?" I looked blank. "Stay there and don't move," he ordered. Five minutes later, he returned with a plate of beans on toast with a banana on top. He fed me like a small child and after an hour or so, I felt better.

We got to bed at 4.30am, and a few hours later I was back in the office striking through another red line on the *Countdown to Pre-trial Review* on the office wall.

This hearing would be pivotal. Had we got enough evidence on our side? A moment later, Paul was with me. "You have your evidence, now it's time to bring in the big guns."

I knew exactly who he meant, and, picking up the phone, I dialled. Would the 'big gun' I was calling want to help?

To my delight, he agreed. "See you in court, Denise," he said.

I called FedEx. "I have 23 boxes full of lever arch files to be delivered to a firm of solicitors in London by 4.55pm on Friday evening. Can you arrange that and ensure signed acceptance of the documents, please?"

Grinning from ear to ear, I wrote a letter asking for a

response to hundreds of questions I had listed and demanded that they send me the answers by Monday morning.

When the courier arrived, it took ten minutes to cart all the boxes of files out to his van. I handed him the letter and watched as he drove off with our nine years of research for the other side's lawyers to turn around in 48 hours.

That evening the three of us sat on the sofa with a bottle of wine I'd been saving for months, toasting one another, and imagining the chaos at the lawyers' offices.

When we arrived outside the court on the morning of the pre-trial review, an army of a Queen's Counsel, barristers, and solicitors, many robed in black gowns and wigs, as centuries-old tradition dictates, had gathered at the other end of the corridor. "Goodness, there must be a lot of court cases going on today," I said.

We settled onto a bench to wait. A moment later every head turned as the double doors swung open with a bang and in strode our secret weapon, the wonderful Charles Purle. Now elevated to Queen's Counsel (he was yet to become a judge – that would happen in 2007, just as I had predicted, when he was appointed as a senior circuit judge and specialist chancery judge), he had answered my plea to come and help – and the grin on his face indicated that he was relishing the battle of wits that lay ahead. "Hello, you gorgeous gal, and not so gorgeous boy," he beamed.

Having studied the law and learned a great deal, I had also prepared five additional amendments to our claims (something traditionally only a trained barrister can do) but I knew the opposition would fight tooth and nail against their inclusion. Somehow, we had to convince the judge. This situation called for Charles; genius in financial and company law with the ability to provide a lightning-fast analysis in any legal situation. Added to which – the icing on our cake – Charles had recently set the precedent on authority and the law of agency, the issue on which our entire case hinged. Legal & General's team now had a real battle on their hands trying to argue against him, also we had the hidden evidence Paul directed me to.

"Charles! Thank you so much for coming." I stood and hugged him.

"Jacobs vs Legal & General," yelled the usher.

We turned to see the lawyers chatting in the corridor snaking their way into the courtroom. I couldn't believe my eyes – all of them had come to fight for Legal & General.

"You've got them more than worried if they need that pack of hyenas to take you on," Charles whispered.

Legal & General's new QC, Julian Malins, sauntered over.

"Hello Charlie, how are things?" he said.

"Well hello, you old bugger. How are you, my lovely ex-brother-in-law?"

Michael and I did a double-take. Brother-in-law?

"He's a pompous windbag," Charles whispered as we filed into court. "He's yet to get the better of me."

The judge entered, dressed in his colourful mediaeval-inspired satin robes and horsehair wig. As he sat, the court fell silent.

"Here we go," Michael nervously murmured as the judge opened the proceedings.

"Good morning. It is incumbent upon me to declare that I have a conflict of interest in this matter."

Glances were exchanged on both sides.

"My wife owns shares in Legal & General," he explained,

"I have a pension with the company."

There was a stunned silence as we all wondered what was coming next.

"I therefore suggest a fifteen-minute recess for you to deliberate if you wish to adjourn today's hearing and return at a later date before a different judge."

With that, he bowed and exited.

All made their way back to the corridor.

"Now what?" I asked Charles as we huddled at one end, whilst Legal & General's cohort occupied the other, wondering what we would do next. Based on their surreptitious glances they must have felt they had the judge onside.

"You couldn't make this up," Charles chuckled, adding, "Denise, if you ever write your life story, make sure this scene is included". Ten more minutes of in-depth debate was eventually interrupted by the usher.

"Jacobs vs Legal & General." She yelled.

"Let's go with it," Charles suggested. The big decision was made.

We all snaked back into court.

"We'll get the buggers," he reassured me after informing Mailins that we would continue with the present judge.

Two tortuous hours later, the judge found in our favour on all my additions. My years in the libraries studying law had paid off.

Once again, the judge surveyed the crowded court.

"Have all discovery documents been exchanged?"

Malins stood up "Yes, My Lord, indeed they have." He scowled at us.

"How say you, Mr Purle?" Charles looked to me and I nodded.

"Everything's in order, My Lord," Charles turned and winked at me.

"Then, I will make an order that the trial be set down four weeks hence at 10.30am."

"They're bound to appeal," Michael mumbled glumly.

Whilst leaving the court, I turned to see a forgotten Tesco carrier bag on a bench. As the door swung shut, leaving me inside, I watched it drift silently to the floor – the lone remnant of an almost ten-year battle for justice.

The following day Charles phoned me. "Denise, I've had a call from my wretched ex-brother-in-law. He must have been on the Wine Gums this morning because he informed me that they are going to make you an offer you can't refuse."

My heart almost missed a beat. "Are you serious?"

"Couldn't be more so, old gal. Looks as though it's game, set and match to you. When they saw the evidence that you had uncovered through Paul, they panicked and paid money into court on a Part 36 basis."

"What's a Part 36?"

"It's a tactical step designed to convince the other party – that's you – to settle the claim early without the matter having to go to court. It's a substantial sum they're offering you in settlement."

"What about all our costs?" I asked, waiting for the catch.

"No catch – Legal & General's offer includes all costs incurred from day one."

"Everyone's?" I asked him.

"Yep. Legal Aid, court costs, your lawyers' fees, my fees, their own legal teams' fees which includes several firms of lawyers and countless barristers and QCs – not to mention my pain in the arse ex-brother-in-law's exorbitant fees. And you get paid for every one of the 9,000 hours you estimate that you have both spent on this case. On top of all that, they have to pay all interest accrued – ouch! Well done to you!

"The only catch is that even though they are throwing all this dough at you, they make no admission of liability. We all know they were in the wrong, but they save face by not having to say so publicly. Can you live with that?"

"What's your advice?" I asked.

"It would have been wonderful to have the opportunity for this case to be heard in open court, as it's about time these financial services scoundrels had their comeuppance, but it's better for you that you settle. By the way, Malins did ask me how you found the evidence."

"What did you say?" I asked.

"I told him it's a complicated story that started when I missed a performance of Swan Lake over 14 years ago," he chuckled. "You've done it, you gorgeously intelligently, weirdly strange woman!"

2018

2 MINUTES TO MIDNIGHT

Failure of world leaders to deal with looming threats of nuclear war. The United States withdraws from Iran nuclear deal

Estimated number of nuclear warheads worldwide:

14,465

CHAPTER NINETEEN

A JOURNEY

Denham Village, September 2002

After I put the phone down, I sat deep in thought. Had we really done it? Was it truly almost over? How could so many different, seemingly unrelated events over so many years have brought us to this extraordinary moment?

"I wish you could make sense of it for me, Paul – how has it all led to this?" I whispered.

A few seconds later, I felt his presence. As with every time he came to me, it was extraordinary. I never, ever got used to it. I never will.

I looked up and saw his face. "Paul," I said. "I can see you." It felt like a moment of pure magic.

He smiled. "You had to take this path, Sis," he said. "And you've done it for the people of the world. We taught you how to see the past and the future. We trained you to sense, to hear, to connect with us and to see the rainbow colours of the soul. Hold my hand and I will remind you of the journey you have taken."

I felt Paul softly take my hand. I wanted to hang on to him and never let him go again.

A second later I felt myself travelling in reverse. A shiver ran down my spine as I watched scientists splitting the atom and then the stricken cities of Hiroshima and Nagasaki. Bodies burned from head to toe, the smell of burning flesh, skin coming away in strips, heads covered in black ash and mouths turned to the sky as acid rain poured down on them.

We moved forward, and I could see myself lying in the bath with baby Daniel on the floor beside me, as Michael's grandpa Jack told me to move the china pitcher. It was the very first time I had heard a voice from the next dimension.

"That was the start, wasn't it?" I whispered, remembering the months I had spent in intense practise after Jack's visit. "The messages started to come through after that."

Next, I saw myself standing in the kitchen watching television. "That was when I asked what the purpose of our existence was," I remembered.

"Yes," Paul said. "And you were given the answer."

"The railway carriages. Celia showed me that we all have a choice about the way we live our lives and choose our routes, we earn our colours, and we have to continue along the track until we learn to give unconditional love." I see myself filling with wonder as Celia told me about the soul and the way our colours shine from it. How powerful that experience had been.

Now we were in our kitchen in Darlington where I was feeding 18-month-old Daniel and I looked out of the window at the terrible nuclear mushroom filling the sky.

"Will it really happen again?" I asked.

"It will," Paul said, "if religious and political leaders do not choose to use power wisely."

A moment later I saw Michael and me, excited about Videocab and our brilliant idea. So full of hope and plans for the future.

The scene changed. I was sitting in a restaurant as Frank raised his glass towards us, and his face turned into that of a toad as he said, "Denise, I'm not interested in your prediction of world war and messages of peace".

"We had taught you to see his true colours," Paul said.

"Yes," I replied. "But no-one believed me."

"That was because the time was not yet right," Paul replied. "In time he revealed his colours, and that is what will happen with all those who wish harm to others."

Then I was watching Nick Montgomery as he was handed the file that, 14 years later, he would send to me. We watched Celia follow him as he walked down to the bottom of his garden, into his office where he placed the file in the eaves amongst hundreds of others.

Now Celia was telling me, "There is a lawyer in Bermuda. Contact him and be very careful not to let Frank know his contact details."

"That was Julian Hall," I said. "He wanted to invest in our company."

"Yes," Paul replied, showing me what happened next. I was on the phone to Anthony, our lawyer who was telling me, "Frank Jarvis has found out about Julian Hall and poisoned the deal. Julian's pulled the plug."

As I replaced the phone, sick with disappointment, Celia told me, "You must phone Julian Hall and invite him to dinner at your home."

I watched myself standing at the front door. "Welcome," I said, kissing Julian on the cheek. He turned to the friend he had brought with him. "This is my accountant and close friend Nick Montgomery."

Over dinner, I heard Celia's voice, "Tell Nick how you saw Frank as a toad and tell him that you are helping us to call for peace, to stop World War Three." So I did, and he said, "I've had a feeling I'd like to put the world to rights too."

As we said our goodbyes, Nick handed me his business card. I watched myself chat to him over the phone the next day. "Your brother Neil wants you to know he is always with you; he will never leave you and he sends his love." All I could hear was the gentle sound of Nick's sobs.

I turned to Paul. "I've only just got it," I said. "All this time, and I was so caught up in dealing with the legal stuff that I never put it all together before. Celia got me to contact Julian so that he could introduce Nick so that Nick could be the one to give me the file 14 years later – right?"

"Of course. Come on, keep up Sis," Paul laughed.

"It's just beyond incredible," I whispered. "How did she do that? How do you manage to be five jumps ahead of us? How do you know that something will be needed in 14 years' time and then set up the trail?"

"You're going to have to wait to find that out when you get here, Sis," Paul smiled.

Then we were at the moment when I saw him for the last time before he left this dimension for the next. I watched as I kissed him gently on his forehead and held his hand in both of mine as he fell asleep.

"Sis, it was a few hours after this that I spoke to you. Remember me explaining that the moment I left my body behind, I could see again, feel the carpet under my feet, move my arms and legs. I could pass through walls, travel to the other side of the world instantly and see the past, present and future?"

I nodded... tearful at the memory of my grief, and then the absolute wonder of hearing the little brother I had just lost speak to me again.

We moved on to Kel Cooper's offices as he handed us his business card. "We at Romford Financial Services are appointed reps of Legal & General. We can arrange a project finance package for your company," he said.

Then Michael and I, sitting in L'Entrecote restaurant as Graham Alexander said, "We need £65,000 as a deposit for the loan." Michael looked aghast, and Kel Cooper smiled, "Don't worry Mike, we can arrange it with an endowment re-mortgage on your property through Carl Fleming of Legal & General."

On we went to our house, where Michael and I were doing the deal with Carl Fleming and Kel Cooper when Annabel appeared. "Carl, last night you moved your old garden bench to the shaded side of your house. Please will you move it back into the sunshine, so that Annabelle can enjoy the warmth of the evening sun again," I was saying to a stunned Carl.

Paul and I watched as, back at Assers, Carl got out of his car and, under a hunter's moon, dragged the bench back to the sunny side of the house.

Back in the restaurant, Graham Alexander was saying, "Congratulations," as he handed us a magnum of champagne. "Contracts will be exchanged tomorrow."

That night Carl Fleming took our green folder from the passenger seat of his car and went inside, where he climbed the right-hand staircase, opened the attic room door and placed the file in a box on the floor.

"We knew you would need this file too, in the future," Paul said. "So, when Carl was about to move to a new house, I told you where to find it before he left."

"Why did I have to have it before he left?" I asked.

"Because this is what happened next," Paul said.

We were standing in Carl's garden as he threw all his old files onto a bonfire. "We know what will happen, and we even know when a beam of sunlight will fall onto a file that you will need one day in the future." Paul told me softly.

He turned to me. "We have taken you on a journey and every single step, every twist and turn, has been a necessary and meaningful part of the whole. I know you suffered and lost so much and wondered what it all meant. But now you can see how it all connected and why every single thing had to happen as it did."

As he slipped away from me, I sat with my head in my hands, weeping tears of sadness and joy, gratitude and loss. I loved him so much, my little brother. And I had been through so much as he and Celia showed me what I had to do and learn and understand. Now, after so many turns in the path, it was almost over.

****

The following day, Legal & General made their offer to settle. We had to decide whether to accept, as Charles and our solicitor, Anthony, both advised.

The decision was taken out of my hands by Paul. "You don't need to spend any more time in court, Sis – it's enough that they are willing to settle with you. You have proved that you were right all along. And you have proved that we in the next world not only exist but know what is going to happen in the future.

"This is not the end. One day we will ask you to tell your story. Then it will be up to those who hear it to save this precious world. But for now, you've earned a rest."

So we accepted the offer, and with our settlement we were able to repay Terry and my parents all they had given to support us.

To celebrate, Michael took me to The Flower Stall outside Uxbridge Underground station and bought me a big, beautiful bunch of red amaryllises.

2020

1 MINUTE 40 SECONDS
TO MIDNIGHT

Continued failure of world leaders to deal
with increased nuclear threat. Heightened
tension between the United States & Iran

Estimated number of nuclear
warheads worldwide:

13,410

CHAPTER TWENTY

THE TIME IS RIGHT

Denham Village 2019

I could hardly take in the news.

"Michael, the book – it's going to happen. And that means the film will happen too. At last. I can't believe it."

It was the spring of 2019. 17 years after the court case had ended it seemed that the next stage of my journey was – finally – about to begin.

Over the years Paul and Celia had told me, many times, that there was more to do – that I would need to get their message out to the world. And they had said that it would happen via a book and a film, and that Dan would compose the film's theme music. "But when?" I would ask them. "And how? What if no-one will listen to me?"

"It will happen when the time is right," Paul said.

Now, it seemed that time had come. A fairy godfather had stepped in to back me and offer his generous support.

We had first met Grahame on one of our regular trips to

Mallorca. He was sitting at the table next to me and Michael, and over a glass of wine or two we swapped stories until 4am. Strangely, after that, we often bumped into him. Paul clearly had a hand in this because we could be driving to one part of the island when I'd hear Paul tell me to head to a different destination - where we would always bump into Grahame. We always enjoyed his company; he'd had a fascinating life and was clever and entertaining.

This went on for some years – just coming across one another in Mallorca, where he was on holiday, stopping for a coffee and a chat and then heading off in our different directions afterwards. It happened so often that I began to wonder; was it just a coincidence, or was there more to it?

One afternoon in 2018, I was just about to go to the beach when I received another message from Paul telling me to see Grahame. Paul said it was urgent, so I sent Grahame a text and he agreed to meet me. As we sat over our coffees, I explained more of my story to him and told him that I was hoping to get a film made.

Grahame sipped his drink thoughtfully and asked me a few questions before disappearing for a few moments. When he returned, he said, "I've just spoken to my lawyer in LA, who says thinking about the film first is the wrong way to go about this. You must get a book written and published, and then the film will follow."

The trouble was, I knew I was not capable of writing a book. I had mastered the art of legal gobbledegook, but a book was a whole different thing. "So now what?" I asked. Paul replied with his usual, "Be patient, Denise. Grahame will help in more ways than one."

A year later, my mobile buzzed.

GRAHAME
Are you sitting down?

DENISE
No. Why?

GRAHAME
I want to help you with the peace project

I stared at my phone, stunned.

DENISE
Don't know what to say! You serious?

GRAHAME
Couldn't be more so

DENISE
But why?

GRAHAME
Because I think you're a good person, I believe in your project and I trust you.

Grahame went on to say that he wanted to fund the book and a website to go with it. I was blown away, but as I sat trying to think what to say, I heard Paul insist I accept Grahame's generous offer. "He's the right person for you to work with. Each of you has been blessed with gifts the other doesn't have. That's why you get on so well together; it's why we arranged for you to meet so often."

"It's just extraordinary," I said to Michael. "Paul said that Grahame would be part of this project and, out of the blue, Grahame says he wants to help. Now I have the funding I'm going to have to do it, but I still have no idea how."

"Well, Paul and Celia are never wrong," Michael said. "We know that much by now. After so many years I know one thing: if they say something is going to happen, then it will."

He was right, of course. I just had to wait, as always, to be shown the next step.

****

So much had happened in the years since the court case concluded in 2002. After the settlement and the pure joy of being able to repay all those who had helped us, Michael and I were eventually able to buy a house around the corner from my parents. By 2008, my mother's dementia had deteriorated, and we could be on hand to help my father care for her.

There were some loose ends that I wanted to tie up in my own mind. One of the most astonishing things about the case had been the messages from Annabelle Towers. So, a few months after the end of the case, I contacted Carl Fleming and asked him if it would be possible for us to see Assers for ourselves.

Carl was charming. He said he would ask the new owners of the house if we could visit, and then invited us to lunch. When we met, a couple of weeks later, he asked us how we were. "I was sorry to hear you lost the case," he said.

"We didn't lose, Carl," I said aghast. "They settled with us, and it cost them a fortune. Who told you that we lost?"

"Legal & General did. They said that you blamed me for

everything going wrong for you."

Michael and I looked at one another and burst out laughing. "That's completely ridiculous," I said. "We had nothing to blame you for – in fact, we were very grateful that you sent us the file just before you moved out because we knew you'd been told not to contact us."

Carl smiled. "Your messages were extraordinary. When I left Assers for the last time, I stood at the front door and said goodbye to Annabelle. I told her that I had left her the garden bench."

That afternoon he took us to Assers, where the new owners had arranged for us to be let in. Carl showed us the two staircases and we walked up the right hand one to the room where the box containing the green file had been kept. He showed me where the beam of sunlight had come through the window, just as Paul had described.

Then he showed me the fireplace the builders had trouble with, before leading me to Annabelle's garden bench, positioned on the sunny side of the garden. It was all just as I had seen it in my mind's eye.

As we left, I could smell the aroma of freshly baked bread and hear the sound of children past, laughing as they crossed the fields.

"Can you believe Legal & General told Carl we had lost the case?" Michael said as we drove home.

"Sadly, I can," I said. "They probably told everyone that we'd lost. The last thing they wanted was news getting out that they'd been caught out by a woman who talks to spirits. It's sad though, because no lessons have been learned. The financial services industry is as corrupt as ever. But it's good to know that Carl didn't know anything about the fraud, and neither did Simon Smith or Kel Cooper, although Kel did break the law by presenting himself as doing business through Legal & General."

It was not long after this that Paul told me that if the financial institutions refused to accept the truth about the state of the financial services industry, and governments allowed things to continue as they were, then it would collapse in a global financial earthquake.

A few years later in 2008, as he had predicted, with the banks' cynical exploitation and shameful practices exposed and many financial institutions falling apart, the world went into a huge recession. Despite this, many bankers got away with it, while people committed suicide and lost everything because of the financial services industry's greed and deceit.

It made no sense to me, but once again Paul reminded me that we all choose our path, which in turn forms our colours.

"This is not about whether you are rich or poor, and it's not about religion or power. This is something all the money in the world cannot buy. And this is the message that everyone in the world needs to understand."

But how was I was going to get people to understand? I still had no idea.

As I waited for more guidance, messages that I needed to pass on to those who needed them continued to come through. One afternoon I arranged to meet some friends; Jonathan Perez, his wife Annette and their two teenage daughters, Mai and Sapir, who I hadn't seen for a long time. We arranged to meet at a café in the Westfield shopping centre in Shepherd's Bush. The place was packed but we found a table and Jonathan and Michael sat together at one end so that they could natter about football and their beloved Chelsea whilst the girls sat at the other end. The girls' conversation was initially driven by the two young teenagers which focused on makeup, shoes, boys, and anything in the colour pink.

I knew that Annette's father had passed on six weeks earlier and as I longingly eyed the chocolate cake placed in front of me, I realised that someone had joined us, and he was desperate to get something off his chest. Oh well, there goes my yummy cake, I thought amused.

I turned to Annette, "Your father is here. He had difficulty with his leg, didn't he?"

Annette's jaw dropped.

"He wants me to tell you that it doesn't hurt anymore, and he is fine now," I continued.

"How... how on earth do you know that?" she asked flabbergasted. But I didn't have time to reply as more messages followed.

"He's telling me that the hospital staff forgot to give you his shoes after he died. You discovered later that they were placed on a ledge under his bed when the room was cleaned."

"Yes," Annette said astonished. "That's right."

Hearing the proof which only her father could have given, Annette knew without a shadow of a doubt that even though we were sitting in a coffee shop in a shopping centre in London, her father's presence was with us.

"Your father is saying that you felt guilty about something that happened a couple of days before his death," I said.

Annette nodded her eyes now full of tears.

"He is asking me to tell you not to blame yourself as it was not your fault."

Annette told me the story. Apparently, it was late evening when the nurse came round to administer medicine to her father. They had begun giving him morphine to help ease the pain, but on this particular evening he pleaded with the nurse not to give it to him. The nurse insisted, saying it would help him have a settled and painless night. In a state of helplessness, he pleaded with his daughter saying, "Annetti, don't let them give me the medicine". But bowing to the superior knowledge of the medical staff, she urged him to take it.

Soon after receiving his dose of morphine, he fell asleep for the final time. He failed to regain consciousness and a couple of days later passed away.

By this time Annette and the two girls were all in tears and nearby diners at other tables were glancing at us. At this point, Jonathan broke from his conversation with Michael and looked across to see his wife and daughters all sobbing, mascara running down three sets of cheeks and the gorgeous chocolate cakes were left wanting.

I then looked at the girls in turn, knowing I had to comfort one of them with a message. It took me a few moments to work out which one it was.

"Sapir, your grandfather is telling me I have to hug you tight, pinch your cheeks for him and give you big kisses on the cheeks," I told her.

Sapir looked startled and then sobbed even more.

Annette revealed that during the final weeks of his life she had visited her father daily in hospital and each time he would ask after all of his grandchildren. At the end he would ask specifically about Sapir, saying that she was mischievous and reminded him of Annette as a little girl. He would tell Annette to give Sapir a big hug, to pinch her cheeks and to give her big kisses on the cheeks. She would always do as he asked and tell both girls what their grandfather had said.

Annette had been left with a burden of guilt after her father's death, and his messages to her lifted that guilt from her shoulders. I was so glad to have been of help.

My own father was, by this time, growing frail and ill and on October 23rd, 2013, he died of cancer. In his final few months Dad had started asking me questions about death. I would explain to him what I'd been taught by Celia and Paul and it comforted him. In a precious moment that I will always treasure, shortly before he died, he said I had been a wonderful daughter and taught him so much.

Just 16 days after my father died, my mother followed him. By that time, she no longer knew any of us – it was heart-breaking and almost too much to absorb. My dear parents, lovable and exasperating in equal degrees, had both gone.

My birthday was four days after Mum's death, and I remember thinking that for the first time in many years I wouldn't receive the birthday bunch of red amaryllises that they always gave me.

Except that I did. That morning Michael took me to The Flower Stall outside Uxbridge underground station where the florist, John, presented me with a huge bunch of red amaryllises, saying, "I don't know why I'm giving these free, but I feel I ought to. If I did this to everyone, I'd be out of business in no time!" And I heard my father's voice saying, "Happy Birthday Denise, with love from Mum and Dad".

It was the confirmation I needed. My parents had reached the world that I knew to be inter-connected with this one, and they had sent me a powerful message. In life they had sometimes doubted me, but now they knew the truth and they wanted me to know it.

At that stage I still had no idea how on earth I was going to get a film of the story made, until one day Paul told me to contact his old friend Philip Bright.

I contacted Philip, who arranged for me to meet his old family friend Sir Sydney Samuelson, the government's first British Film Commissioner and a giant in the film industry. Sir Sydney, who was charming, said that the best way to get a film idea up and running was to get someone in the business to help me.

Soon after this, I was introduced to film producer Iain Smith. Iain had produced a string of hugely successful films, including *The Killing Fields*, *Seven Years in Tibet* and *Cold Mountain*. He turned out to be a lovely man. He took me under his wing and taught me how to write scripts, and all about the process of getting a film made. And I was introduced to Jonny Persey of the Met Film School, who helped me by arranging a scriptwriting course which has been invaluable during the writing of this book.

Steps were falling into place, but I still didn't have a way to bring about the film until one day I bumped into Jonathan Blair, nephew of Michael's old friend Jeff. Many years earlier whilst Jonathan was at university, planning to study accountancy, he visited our home. Over a cup of coffee, I received a message for him saying, "You're not going to be an accountant as you're intending to be," I said, "You're going to end up being an entertainment lawyer."

He hadn't believed me at the time, but years later he had indeed become a successful entertainment lawyer, so he knew that the messages I received were genuine. After a warm reunion, Celia urged me to tell him the whole story.

Jonathan told me that he would do what he could to

help. He got investment funding, then put me together with a production company. Contracts were signed, and the task of writing the screenplay with a professional writer began. But progress was slow and eventually we realised that it just wasn't working.

"The scriptwriter has basically written about a court case, and this story is about so much more than that," Jonathan said in one production meeting. "It's about the extraordinary messages Denise has received and making a big impact on the consciousness of humanity to tell them that we are heading for a nuclear disaster. We need to attract the finest filmmakers and this script won't do that."

As harsh as his professional opinion was, I knew he was right, so I parted company with the production house. I was disappointed, but I knew this was not the end of the journey. "Jonathan, it's not over," I told him. "I've seen this happen many times. We're just being shifted in a different direction. It will work out for the best, you'll see." Although, I had no idea what that different direction would be.

Sadly, Jonathan's uncle Jeff had become very ill by this time. One day when he was with us, I said, "Jeff, I know you thought I was misguided and wrong in my beliefs. Do you still believe that?" He answered, "No. I was wrong about you". He gave me a huge hug, which meant so much to me that I shed a few tears.

For the next couple of years, I waited to see what would happen next. And then came Grahame's advice to write the book first, followed by his generous offer to fund it.

I talked to Jonathan and he advised me to put together a timeline, from the very start of my story right through to the ending of the court case. It took me many months, using

Michael's diaries and our joint recollections and accounts, but I ended up with a document that I knew would be the springboard for my book.

Next, I found an experienced editor, the wonderful, patient, open-minded and talented wordsmith Caro Handley. She helped me turn the chronology into a real book – and we had a lot of fun doing it. At the same time, the website was created, with Dan's beautiful and haunting music to accompany it.

As I worked on my book, I thought about the many incredible messages I have been given over the years and what being able to receive them has meant in my life. I had never looked for or expected to have the ability to hear and see messages from the next dimension. Why me? I will never know. But I have learned and understood so much, and for that I feel very blessed.

Some people are able to communicate with those who have passed on from this world to the unseen dimension surrounding us, and others can't. It seems as simple and as puzzling as that. And it is another world, whether we like it or not. We are all destined to go to it when our lifespan here comes to an end and its energy envelops us in the same way that the ocean envelops a fish. Fish can't see the world of water they live in, just as we can't see the air surrounding this world in which we exist.

The fish analogy is a good one. When we see startled fish escaping from predators, we can see their past and the direction they are rushing towards - their present and future. It is a doomed future if they are caught in the trawlers' nets, or a better future if they change direction and escape their death. We can see these events by looking into the water, as we are outside it. And it's similar for those in the next dimension. They can see our past, present and future in the same way that we can see the journey of a fish.

All of us genuine mediums and psychic people are no different to anybody else. We all have our lives to live, we all make our own personal mistakes, as we too have been put here to learn. The good and the not-so-good happen to every single one of us.

Why is it that just because we can receive messages, we should be given a life any different to anybody else's? I look at it from a different perspective, in that it can sometimes be a real pain, but on the other hand it can also be mind-blowingly extraordinary.

Take the warm summer day, not long ago, when Michael and I walked along the South Bank of the Thames in London, up to Westminster Bridge, past the Houses of Parliament, the river boats plying their trade and the London Eye, its carousels reflecting the sun, on towards the Oxo Tower and the Tate Modern. The South Bank was milling with the locals and with tourists from all over the world enjoying the beautiful day and what London had to offer.

We headed on towards Borough Market, a vibrant, colourful market where we wandered amongst the stalls, crammed with displays of fruit and vegetables, foods, spices, herbs, breads and cheeses.

The other side of the market meandered onto the street where we stopped at a florist. Venus flytraps hung from the ceiling, and we caught the heady scent of lilies and jasmine. The extraordinary magic of flowers never ceases to astound me.

Then I heard Paul's voice. "Look up, Sis."

I looked up to see what appeared to be a white balloon shape floating towards the sky as if heaven bound. It morphed into an exquisite iridescent white mass of energy that grew larger and larger. As it grew millions of ribbons of shimmering white light extended from it and I watched as they attached to the solar plexus of every single person in the crowds around me.

I could see the rainbow of colours forming around each person. These were the colours we all earn. The blues, greens, yellows, oranges, reds, purples, and browns. Every single person in the market was attached to this extraordinary shape in the sky. I knew in that moment that we truly are all brothers and sisters regardless of skin colour, creed, gender or religion and we all have a choice about how we use our power throughout our designated life.

2021

1 MINUTE 40 SECONDS TO MIDNIGHT

Continued modernisation of nuclear arsenals globally

Estimated number of nuclear warheads worldwide:

Unknown

Four years to prevent the Doomsday Clock reaching midnight…

CHAPTER TWENTY-ONE

REVELATIONS FROM THE NEXT DIMENSION

Denham Village 2020

Do Paul and Celia want anything more added to this book, I wondered as I held the pill box Paul had given me just before he died? It was one of my most precious possessions, and in the years since my little brother left this world I had often thought of his words when he gave it to me.

This little gold and mother-of-pearl box contained just a few pound coins, but it was the last thing Paul had that belonged to him, and he told me that it would be our secret code, a way for me to contact him. Now I looked at it and asked him, "Have I put everything into my book that you wanted me to say, Paul? Is there anything more?"

A moment later the room was filling with a luminous golden haze and I knew he was with me.

"Remember when I gave you that box?" he asked.

"How could I forget?" I exclaimed.

"At that time, I never expected it to be a part of a book," he said, smiling. "There is a little more to add to the story now. And it is the most powerful message of all. So, take the coins and hold them tightly in the palm of your hand."

I did as he said, holding the coins in my hand and focusing with all the energy and concentration that I knew I would need in order to understand what he was about to show me.

Once again, Paul took my hand and I felt myself pulled back in time with a rush and an energy that told me we were going a long, long way back. A moment later I found myself floating in a dense and silent black void. I could just about make out a mist which began pouring into the blackness from all sides.

As it grew, there was an eerie silence until the mist began to swirl faster and faster as I floated on, until I was confronted by a gargantuan swirl of energy, in the centre of which formed a titanic mass of rock that shone and sparkled in a cornucopia of colours from black to gold, silver and diamond white.

The sheer brilliance of the colours was blinding. I knew that this mass was made up of gases which hissed like a pressure cooker as the concentration in the core intensified until it could not be contained any more. The outcome was an explosion so huge and so loud that it defies description, and the effects of which continue today and will continue into eternity.

Paul had shown me the creation of our universe.

The mist then receded into the unseen to wait for the billions of years until the first homo sapiens would walk the Earth, when that same mist would infuse us with our human souls.

"Now open your hand," Paul said.

I opened my hand and watched the coins ascending from my palm as they spread into different areas of the room. These were the planets of our solar system. Our own planet Earth gradually became a tiny pinprick as our universe expanded further and further around me.

"Ever since the beginning of humankind, we have looked to the night sky," Paul said. "We marvel at the stars and planets we see, wondering how it all came about. Well, the universe was not made by accident; it is our home, and every single part of it has a purpose. Science has learned a lot, but no living being will ever fully understand how it was created. Every planet, every star, every black hole is there for a reason – to enable our existence here on this earth.

"The sun is positioned at the precise distance from our planet to keep us warm and give us the light we need for every living creature and plant to survive. Any closer to the earth, we would all burn. Any further away, we would freeze. This is not chance or coincidence.

"The same applies to our moon and every other planet that surrounds us – they all have energy fields that affect one another. Scientists, with their tremendous advancements in astrophysics, are just beginning to understand the purpose of black holes. They are vital to our existence; their profound energy props up the universe and forms shortcuts between one part of the vast cosmos and the next. These black holes prevent the universe from collapsing inwards or pulling too far apart. Think of them like cosmic scaffolding," he chuckled.

"Everything is linked. Every atom is connected by energy, vibration and colour in our world. And our world is in turn linked with the next dimension."

What Paul said reminded me of a quote I once read from

Chief Seattle, a leading figure among the North American Suquamish and Duwamish people:

> *"Humankind has not woven the web of life. We are but one thread within it. Whatever we do to the web, we do to ourselves. All things are bound together. All things connect."*

I was filled with wonder at what Paul had shown me. And I knew there was more. The luminous glow of his presence shone powerfully in the room.

"Tell me about what happens when we die," I whispered.

I knew from what Celia and Paul had previously shown me that when our heart stops beating, our soul, together with all the colours it has earned, detaches itself from its home in our body. Paul put it this way: "Think of the soul as a driver who gets out of their car".

"And then what?" I asked.

"Once the soul is separated from the body, we are simply a mass of energy, like everything else in the universe. When that happens you can't see us," Paul said, "but we can see you. That's because the vibrations in the next dimension are much faster – yours in the world where you are now are denser and slower.

"But our two worlds are interlinked; the next dimension surrounds yours. Imagine this as an invisible web which surrounds every part of the physical dimension and which is quite miraculous. A place we are all destined to return to when we die."

"Wherever and whenever we are born, we must all live what is mapped out for us. And when our allotted time is up, we return to this dimension, which is our home."

"And then?" I asked. "What next?" I, like so many others, had always wanted to know whether after we die, we come back to this earth again. "Do we return in a different body? Is reincarnation what really happens?" I asked him.

"It is," Paul replied. "We have all been here before, and we will all come back again."

My head was spinning. I was learning the most extraordinary things.

"So, this means you are coming back?" I asked. "And Celia? And if you are both going to come back, that must mean that you are afraid not just for our future but for your own."

"Yes," Paul replied. "We don't want to return to a world that has been destroyed by the foolishness and selfishness of a few who hold power. The world is so precious, it will sustain all of us for all of time if we only care for it and protect it."

"Oh, my goodness," I whispered. "I never realised this before. Stopping nuclear war is not just for us, for the children here now – it is for all of us in the future when we return."

Paul smiled sadly. "You've got it, Sis. If the world is blown up, it will lead to future generations blighted by sickness, many of them with short, painful lives, everyone in a desperate struggle to find food and shelter and to survive."

I paused as this terrible scenario unfolded before my eyes. Scenes of heartbreak and bleakness, of dry earth and makeshift shelters, of babies born with deformities and ill health.

The revelation that we have all been here before and we are all coming back had been hinted at by Celia when she showed me the railway carriage, but now it absolutely blew my mind. Who had I been? Who would I be? Who would any of us be – and why?

"You want us to explain all about it, don't you?" Paul said.

I nodded, using everything I had ever learned about receiving messages in order to hear what he was telling me.

"Each of us has one soul," he said. "Some souls are older than others. Some are brand new. There are infinite numbers of souls miraculously created by the great mass of interconnecting energy you witnessed that day in Borough Market, the energy that links us all.

"When we are born, we are here to learn, to experience situations we have earned, both good and bad," Paul said. "These lessons are from our previous incarnations, sometimes spanning many thousands of years. If we hurt anyone, in any way, we will have to learn from the experience and not make the same mistakes in our next life. This is how it works.

"In other words, we die and leave our bodies, then there's a different kind of existence after death, and then, hey presto, we will be coming back to put right our actions. Don't you love the magic of it all?"

I couldn't help but laugh. When he was with us in life, he always had the knack of making the serious sound funny, and he could still do it even from the next dimension. But what he was telling me was deadly serious and hugely significant for the way we choose to lead our lives.

"So, must we continue to come back forever?" I asked.

"No," Paul replied. "Life is all about learning, growing and evolving until our souls reach purity and glow white. Once this has been achieved, we do not need to return to the physical world again. I'm still working on it," he added, making me smile again.

"We all come from the next dimension, and we will all

return there. There is no other dimension than these two; where you are now and where I am now. In your dimension you can have all the pleasures that come with having a body, like enjoying food. But you can also grow sick or be injured.

"Where I am now, in the afterlife, it is impossible to describe other than to say it just is, and it's natural for us all to be here because it's our home. There is no physicality here. And there is no payback in the next dimension, it is a place of love. The consequences of our actions in this life come upon our return when we are given a new body and a new journey to live and experience.

"When we are in the physical world, our former loved ones watch over us until we join them, or until they return to the earth dimension once more."

Stunned by the magnitude of what I was hearing, I reached for a chair and sank onto it. After a minute or two, I looked at the luminous glow that told me Paul was still with me.

"Can I ask you some more questions?" I said, "There's so much I've always wondered about."

"Yes," he said. "Ask me. If I can tell you then I will."

This is how I learned the following:

Our new body does not resemble our old one, but where we are born is not down to chance; we will be reborn close to the place where we lived at the end of our life.

We can't choose our parents; they are chosen for us by the power that connects us all.

We don't meet the same people in every new life, but soulmates – a special person with whom we share a deep connection – do exist in any single lifetime.

If you die with a certain talent, it will return with you in your next journey. But if you have a fear, addiction or a compulsion, it will not return with you, and if you die traumatically it doesn't affect your next life.

We are reincarnated over numerous lives until we reach purity. The number of lives we may have is limitless. Every time we return, it is to learn not to make the same wrongs. When the population increases, new souls, with blank canvases, begin their journey.

Animals do not have souls, only humans do, so we can't come back as animals.

"So, I'm not coming back as next door's annoying cat then?" I teased.

"No," he grinned. "You're safe from that."

"But none of us is safe from being blown to pieces in a nuclear war – and then coming back to a world that is barren and burned and filled with radiation?"

"No – none of us is safe from that."

I thought about what Paul was telling me. Children, perhaps him and Celia and so many others, would be born to those who survive the dreadful ravages of nuclear fall-out. Generations of those souls would return to earth, and their lives would be a living hell.

What right does anyone have to destroy their future? What harm have these souls done to be born disfigured and maimed? What have these souls done to inherit a world destroyed by nuclear fallout in the name of greed, and absolute power?

What right does any individual have to kill for their own agenda? What kind of person believes they are doing the right thing by destroying countless lives and futures?

Nuclear weapons today are thousands of times more powerful than those which fell on Japan at the end of World

War Two. Each generation has created more dangerous weapons than those that went before. If one of these weapons is discharged now then the world will be faced with a hurricane of fire sweeping over us at over 5,000 degrees centigrade, vaporising hundreds of thousands of people. There will be carnage on a scale that is unimaginable, creating a worldwide human graveyard.

"Paul – how do I get across the warning that such destruction threatens all of us? What will it take to achieve sense and a vote for peace?"

"You must warn everyone of the truth," he said.

My solar plexus felt as though it would burst with pain and sadness.

The shimmering light in the room intensified and I knew it was time for Paul to leave.

"I'll do whatever I can to warn everyone," I said. "I won't break my promise. I just pray that people will listen."

"I know you will, Sis," Paul said.

"This book will tell them everything you have said and everything you have taught me," I promised him.

"It's now up to you to decide your future. Tell all those who read your book that it's about the love in our souls," Paul said. "Together we can all use our collective power for the good of humanity and of our world. And tell them to think of the children. Their future – our future – is in their hands."

WITNESS STATEMENTS

There are many more testimonies to include but I hope this provides enough examples.

John Cradduck
Bill Blass
Marilyn Macaluso
Janet West
Sue Rule
Nick Montgomery
Liz Longley
Anthony Fiducia
Philip Bright
Deborah Bright
Jonathan Perez
Annette Perez
Terry Bilton
Richard V. Colan, M.D., S.C.
Assers
Michael Jacobs
His Honour Judge Charles Lambert Purle QC (deceased)

JOHN CRADDUCK

It was the end of a seemingly ordinary day at work when I first met Denise and Michael. We were all set to pack away our floral display when I struck up a conversation with the pair as they warmed up with a coffee next to my stall. We discussed the positives and negatives that present themselves when working outdoors, and the trials and tribulations of hairdressing.

It's very rare that I give away flowers, as we work by such a small profit margin, but something, (I can't explain it) made me feel that I wanted to give some to Denise. I chose a beautiful bouquet, wrapped them and handed them to her.

After I gave them to her, Denise asked what flowers they were, as they hadn't opened yet, to which I answered, "Amaryllis". She asked me if they were red, and I said yes – I often had white ones but had only been able to get red that week.

Denise reacted with what I can only call utter disbelief and shock. She told me that as I handed her the flowers, she could hear her father's voice saying, "Happy Birthday Denise. With love from Mum and me".

It turned out that Denise's parents, who had both passed away just days earlier, would always treat her to red amaryllis on her birthday. As they were unfortunately no longer with us, Denise wouldn't have received these as she had every year. So my simple gesture was personified in its meaningfulness.

The Flower Stall is a big one, with vases of every flower imaginable. I had no way of knowing, when I picked the red amaryllis from one of the numerous vases, that Denise's parents would buy her these particular flowers, only ever red and only ever on this special day. Needless to say, she was very touched by the gesture and took great comfort in knowing that somehow her parents had managed to ensure her vase was filled with flowers of such sentimental significance even after their passing.

We have stayed friends ever since, as Denise feels such a connection and a shared love of red amaryllis.

I found this story so extraordinary that when I got home, I told my wife. Her reaction was to say that they must have been sent to Denise from heaven.

The Flower Stall
Uxbridge Underground Station
March 2018

BILL BLASS

I met Denise Jacobs through a friend in Darlington. I was always very cynical about people who purported to be able to communicate with the departed. I was convinced they could not be authentic or were taking advantage of other people's vulnerability.

The thought that anyone could speak to those who had died was beyond what I believed to be credible. So while I thought Denise was great, I didn't take her 'gift' seriously.

It was around 1984 that I decided it was time to take on a new challenge. The opportunity to start afresh as a partner in a joint retail venture in the London area seemed a much more attractive proposition and worth a go.

One day, Denise called into the shop to find a new pair of jeans, when out the blue she gave me a message she had received – that I was going to move to London, and I was going to be changing my job from fashion to electronics.

My jaw dropped with amazement because no-one knew I was about to leave my job and move away to London. But working in electronics could not have been further from my mind, as my experience had always been in clothing manufacturing and retail.

Then things took a strange turn. The retail shop did not work out for me, and I used to bump into a chap who boasted that his nephew was making a fortune selling computers. This was an area I knew nothing about, but I thought that maybe it was worth investigating

The end result is that for the last 33 years I have been working in electronics. So, Denise was absolutely right.

When my wonderful Mum passed away in 2008, I was devastated. I phoned to tell Denise my sad news. Denise tried to console me, and a couple of days later she phoned me when I was about to go to Mum's funeral and feeling very low. She told me to cheer up and that Mum was with her, wanting to tell me she was fine.

I asked Denise how she could prove the message was from my mum. Denise told me Mum wanted to say that she loved Custard Creams. These were her absolute favourite biscuits, she adored them, and there was no way Denise could ever have known that. This eased my distress, and it gave me so much comfort knowing that Mum was still around me.

Denise phoned to make sure I was okay after the funeral, and she told me Mum was with me. I asked Denise to give me proof, and she said I had Mum's glasses with me on the coffee table. This was true and I was speechless.

I feel so very grateful to Denise. Her messages went a long way to helping me through this bereavement. As I travel down life's highway it gives me enormous satisfaction to know that sometimes Mum is with me. Every time something good happens, I look up to the sky and smile!

Denise is one in a million.

Middlesex
July 2019

MARILYN MACALUSO

When someone close to you dies, you find yourself clinging to every last vestige of memory. You so want one more conversation, a letter, a word, or... something.

With that in mind, I sat at my friend Denise's kitchen table and wished and hoped that just maybe I would get some sort of message from my dad William, who had passed away not long before, in March 1992.

This was the second time I'd sat in anticipation of hearing something significant from the ether, the 'other side', our dearly departed – who knows who or what? The thing to understand here is that although Denise says the words, she's under instruction – hearing things, if you will. She doesn't make it up; she tells it like it is. Or doesn't, which means that sometimes, people don't hear what they *want* to hear.

On this particular day, our mutual friend Janet West was also with us, looking on as I made some notes. Denise seemed to 'acknowledge' someone or something and she said my dad was 'here'. Then she began looking for something, opening kitchen drawers and asking Michael to help.

Eventually she found what she wanted – a pen – and she sat and wrote something down. When she passed it over, it was my father's signature, written in green ink. That was my 'wow' moment – my father preferred a fountain pen, and he always used green ink.

My father's old passport happened to be in my handbag. I got it out and showed Denise the signature – it was exactly as she had written it. This was really amazing and true proof of all that she had said. There is no way she could have had any idea whatsoever of my father's use of green ink for his signature. It was an unforgettable moment, and one that I feel incredibly lucky to have witnessed.

Denham

February 2018

JANET WEST

I met Denise outside the school our children attended. The first time I met her, she approached me pointing to my three-year-old daughter, who was waiting with me for her big sister. She asked, "Is that your little girl?" Denise then informed me that my daughter was allergic to the aluminium that can usually be found in tap water.

I was astounded. My daughter was suffering from severe eczema, and that very afternoon I had attended a hospital for treatment. At this appointment, I was told to buy her bottled water and only to give her very quick showers. The consultant suggested that she was likely to be allergic to the allergens in simple tap water.

I asked Denise how she knew. Denise said, "I just know". I told her of my appointment, and she confirmed that the consultant was correct in her diagnosis with regard to tap water. Consequently, my daughter did not drink tap water again.

Some years later during the late 1990s, I was invited along with another friend, Marilyn Macaluso, and our children to Denise and Michael's home for a cuppa after school.

As Michael was making the tea and the five children played, Marilyn asked Denise if she could say anything about her father who had recently passed away. Denise was silent but got up from her seat at the table. She began to open drawers as if she was looking for something. As I remember, Michael asked what she was looking for, but Denise did not talk. She continued opening different drawers and rifled through them until she eventually held up a pen.

She took a scrap piece of paper and began writing. It

was the signature of Marilyn's father, written in green ink. Marilyn stared at it, and then took an old black passport from her handbag and turned to the signature.

Marilyn's father's signature neatly matched the scrawled writing on Denise's scrap paper. Furthermore, Marilyn's father had only ever written in green ink. All three of us were in awe. Denise said that she just knew she needed to find a green pen with which to write.

Although over the years, I have forgotten many things, this moment has always stayed with me. I always wondered how it could possibly be that Denise would actively seek out a green pen, seemingly not really knowing why she needed a pen that was specifically green. And why did Marilyn have her father's passport in her handbag that afternoon? I will never know.

It remains unexplained, but somewhat comforting that in those incredible moments that Denise touched my life, she did "just know".

Middlesex
February 2018

SUE RULE

I first met Denise in a table tennis hall, where we had gone to watch our sons playing in a tournament in 1995. We became good friends.

Almost a year after Dad's passing, Denise asked me and Mum to come over for a cup of tea. Dad spoke to Mum through Denise and he told us lots of things to prove it was him. He describes mum crying a lot and looking at photos, and thinking that his death was all such a waste.

She never had to do anything; he always looked after her and dealt with all the finances and paperwork. He told Mum she was needed as a mother and person – and to let go and get on. "You are not hopeless, you are here. It's not your time"

He knew that Mum would do anything to say goodbye and have a cuddle. He told her, "You were the most wonderful mother, woman, nurturer and wife one could ever have. Everything you did in the house was perfect everywhere." He described the school days of me and my sister; how I was too much of a perfectionist and my sister was more relaxed. He described how he had bad neck rash from his starched collars, and then asked, "Now do you believe it's me?"

He said, "I was very aggressive and impatient, you know. It was part of the job and became a habit". And he added, "A massive cuddle to Sue to make up for the ones I didn't give".

Denise suddenly saw a grey shape; about 5ft 10inches, rounded shoulders but standing correctly. It was Dad; he turned towards Mum, kissed her on her cheek, took both her hands and knelt. "I love you," he said. "You are the love of my life. No one will ever replace you. Thank you for being there throughout our married life, through thick and thin. I am sorry for all the aggravation I gave you. You took it and never said a word."

No-one else saw him, but I felt a sudden presence of heat in the room.

Denise had never met my parents and was totally unaware of their personalities or home life, yet she captured true traits and events that she could only have been told through messages.

Sometime later, after Mum had passed away, my sister and I had a big falling out. I went to see Denise to seek advice, and had 10 questions in my bag written down to ask her. I didn't even need to get them out, as messages came through answering every one of them before I could ask.

Denise gave me messages from Mum and Dad. They were trying to resolve the situation with my sister, and I was told what to write to her.

I was really scared to do it, fearing it would cause more upset. But I trusted Denise's messages and went ahead and wrote the letter, taking many deep breaths! It resulted in the problem being resolved, and we haven't looked back since.

I hope this gives a true insight into the wonderful gift that Denise has. She has been such a big help to me during very difficult times in my life. I totally trust and believe in everything she has told me over the years, and it's interesting to read back over my notes to see how things have worked out as she said. Denise is a great comfort to me. There is no way she would have been able to describe people, events and places without having messages from souls departed.

London
January 2018

NICK MONTGOMERY

Denise, you asked me to revisit the past and in particular the part I played in the story of how you won your court case against Legal & General.

I say, "the part I played," but really, I carried on in my mysterious ways, and you carried on in your particularly mysterious ways. The two mysterious ways collided and uncovered the missing evidence to prove your case in a way some might have difficulty in believing.

No worries there, however, because the facts in the case show it did happen. Any lawyer building a chronology of events would agree with what happened. They might struggle with the "How?" But the strange and magical "Why?" is that all the roads led to you meeting me. I would be the one to provide you with the evidence to win the case against Legal & General. Finding Julian Hall in Bermuda was your key to finding me and winning the case.

The backdrop to our meeting and the subsequent revelations goes back to my childhood in India. I was born in Calcutta and I was always a very challenging child; not that I challenged anyone. I just wanted to be left alone, particularly by grown-ups.

I had a brother, Neil. He was two years older than me, and we were very close. When I was five, Neil went to boarding school in England, leaving me on my own. I had been given a carpentry set and I remember banging together an aeroplane so I could escape and join him. It was big enough to sit in, it but sadly it didn't move.

Another two years on, and I joined Neil. With our parents

in India, they were entirely reliant on the school to ensure their sons were brought up sensitively and in a way that would help prepare them for the life to come.

That was fine for Neil, a normal child in every sense of the word. For me, the school never managed to arrive at the sensitive bit or prepare me for anything. Their challenge was managing a person who came with his own set of rules and dystopian view of life.

Even though my brother and I were polar opposites, the bond shone with searing strength whenever I got into trouble. Neil, intelligent, caring and communicative, became a protective force field around me. He persuaded the headmaster not to beat me, standing in the background preventing catastrophe as many dire events unfolded. That continued into public school until he was killed tragically in 1966, when I was 15.

After this life-changing event, the virtual world I had created as a child merely extended and Neil remained with me as if he were still alive. I ran a lot, and when I ran, I imagined Neil was with me.

I was also interested in music, and I went on to form a band and perform. When I moved to London, I advertised for a singer in the Melody Maker. I received many replies, and one was from Julian Hall, who was over from Bermuda, studying law. We were soon singing and recording together, a close relationship that continued until his recent death.

My career took many different paths, from Deloitte (a firm of accountants in London) to trading and electronic companies.

It was Julian who contacted me and said he would like me to meet you and Michael. He said he was planning to invest in your Transport Media project. Julian also rather sheepishly told me that you were a medium, probably not wanting to commit himself either way as to what this actually meant or whether he believed in it.

From my perspective, my world was constructed on parallel and spiritual paths, so there was no question in terms of belief.

I went with Julian and met you and Michael. Sam Smith was also there. He had a banking background in Bermuda and had ideas about setting up his own loan finance operation in the UK. As well as initiating various projects with Sam Smith, conversations continued with you and Michael.

Also, around the same time, I set up my own company, Cadland Limited. With Julian I had learnt to deal effectively with legal matters, and I had particular skills around accounting, planning and database management. The gales of 1989 had knocked down a cow shed in the garden, and I used the foundations to build a new office, with a music and filing centre at the back.

I remember sitting in the office and working through figures that you and Michael had given me. I had some questions, so I rang you, and when we spoke you told me that Neil was with me and that he would never leave me. You told me that my office was filled with toys from my childhood. You told me about the yellow submarine toy I'd loved in India, and the white umbrella my mother used to protect herself from the sun. You talked about the music and how it was important to me.

Anyone who might have known about the yellow submarine was dead. Few people knew I had anything to do with India, and all the evidence pointed to me not having a brother, but just a sister. I put my head in my hands and cried uncontrollably. The virtual world I lived had transformed into an actual world. When I ran, Neil ran.

Time progressed with the Transport Media project. No-one ever gave up. Each problem was addressed and resolved one way or another; that is, before the Legal & General case and its 12 lawyers. By this stage you had become very thin, and you were very thin anyway. There seemed no way out. I believe you begged for help from the dearly departed. You were clearly having problems continuing and needed help.

It was then that you received a message to ring me. For me, the call was totally out of the blue. There was no reason for you to ring me apart from you being told to, on the basis that I would have the evidence that would win you the case against Legal & General and that it would be in a brown file.

Well, I had lots of brown files! This wasn't a hoarding thing, it was precautionary. I was a little confused about Legal & General, as I really never had any dealings with insurance companies. While believing you that I did have the evidence, my mind was entirely blank as to where it might be.

You had no knowledge of my diligent filing regime, or that I knew anything about Legal & General that might be useful to you. Neither did I, for that matter! I dug up all the files that might have any association with you which included my dealings with Sam Smith and his associates. This included projects selling tents, freezer vans and forming Finance Express.

I found a brown file with references to Legal & General in my dealings with Kel Cooper and his company. It was curious that this brown file contained the letter you needed, as it really did not seem that relevant to what I was doing. I sent this file to you, and I think other items were also useful to you; hand-written notes and original letters.

The unbelievable truth is that you had been given a message in 1987 which enabled you to meet me in anticipation of me providing you with the evidence you needed in 2002, 15 years later.

West Sussex

2018

LIZ LONGLEY – SISTER OF
NICK MONTGOMERY

Notes from reading of Denise Jacobs to Liz Longley, March 1995

My father died on January 21st, 1995. I was 30 and it hit me very hard. He had always been my rock and it was a very difficult time for me. I would wake up at night and could not sleep. Gradually, over a period of time, I became aware of the curtains in our bedroom moving although the windows were closed. I kept hearing the name 'Denise, in my head. I knew my brother Nick had a friend called Denise who was a medium, but no more.

Eventually I rang Nick and said that – although this was incredibly weird – would it be possible for me to talk to Denise? I went to see her, and she gave me a long reading, with all kinds of information about my family, my brothers and parents.

Here is the rough transcript of part of the reading that she gave me, with my father passing messages through her.

"Liz does not like new dark loo seat, irritates her as well as the chrome handle" – this made the reading real for me. All the other things were true, but possibly could have been known. This was not! Jonathan had replaced a loo seat, and I HATED it! I did not want to admit it as I did not want to hurt his feelings. The bathroom was all pine, and the loo seat was mahogany! Made me smile! I had told no one about this.

"Dad is with Neil and can see, he's very, very, happy" – my father was blind, so this was lovely to hear. Also, that he was with my brother Neil, who died when he was 17, my brother

Nick was 15 and I was 18 months old.

"Mum, you are not wearing your engagement ring" – this was true at that time.

"Mum cannot settle, cannot sleep, and must take brandy to sleep. Drinks out of balloon" – all true at the time.

"Mum is lonely" – she was.

"Mum – thank you for all the love and help with baths and dressing, can't wait for you to join me" – self-explanatory, my Mum had looked after him in his last illness, and they loved each other very much.

"Mum must realise how lucky she is, she has wonderful children" – But of course!

"Liz not going to be next" – I was sure I was going to die imminently after my father's death.

"Liz paranoid about hospitals" – exactly right. I hate them to the point that I had my first daughter at home, and only had my second in hospital as she was early. I did have to be convinced that I was not going to die, even then!

"Liz you must pull yourself together otherwise you will have a nervous breakdown – accept things, do not worry, everything is mapped out" – I was in a real mess after my father died. Coming to see Denise really was a turning point.

"Liz waking up at night curling away from husband, looking at the stars and moon" – yes, I did.

Oxfordshire

2018

ANTHONY FIDUCIA

Denise,

Soon after I started to act as your lawyer, many years ago, you told me at one of our first meetings that my father was a doctor, when we had never discussed him.

You also said that he had died, (I was then a young man), again a fact that we had never discussed.

I recall being astounded at how on earth you could have known these facts.

Best wishes,

Anthony

PHILIP BRIGHT

"Come on, Paul, you've got to be joking. What do you mean your sister is a medium? You know I need to see someone who can sort out this bloody mess I'm in, not some charlatan with a load of tea leaves."

"No, honestly – she's amazing and she will know what to do."

"But I told you I need a lawyer, a counsellor, at least someone who works in Citizens' Advice – not some madwoman. What the hell can she do?"

"You'll be surprised what she knows. Just give her a chance. After all, what else can we do on a Saturday morning?"

So that's how I came to meet Denise Jacobs, a person who not only changed my whole thought process, but who supported me, comforted me, guided me and became one of my best friends. Paul was right – she did know what to do!

It was back in July 1991 when things came to a head in my marriage and confused and emotional, I needed to talk to someone.

A day or two later I went to Paul Bilton, one of my dear friends, to see if he knew a lawyer who could advise me about what my options were. That's when Paul took me Denham to meet his sister.

Denise had the tea and biscuits ready, and immediately upon meeting her I felt relaxed by her soft voice, warmth and sensitivity. I thought, "Well, let's do this. After all, what have I got to lose?"

So we retreated to the lounge, where Denise started to tell me all about myself, who I really was, what I felt and how I regarded things. She exposed my inner self, the persona we all keep to ourselves, hidden from public and even from those of our friends and family who we hold closest and who are at the very core of our trust. This started to unnerve me a little.

She went on to do the same about my wife, and then described my home to a tee. Then out of the blue she blurted, "It won't last". How did she know about what was going on? Had Paul said something (he swore not) about the issues my wife and I were having?

Denise then went into detail about my wife and what was happening in our lives.

How did she know this? Lucky guess? Someone told her? Possibly – but who if it wasn't Paul or me? Anyway, this didn't prove anything. So, on she went...

"Your immediate boss will be made redundant, but you are OK. There is a man (whose initials she then gave me) who will always be there for you." My MD had these very initials but why would he always be there for me?

"No," she said. "It's someone connected to your business, but not in this business, who has fingers in lots of pies". At the time I had no idea who she was talking about. Subsequently, over the years, my mentor, with those initials, has always come up trumps just when I have needed him in so much of my career, for which I will forever be grateful.

"In six months, you will be happy, and in two years you will be happier than ever," she said.

I kept testing her, asking for more details, and with each question she had a detailed response that only I could know or understand.

Now, all through this, it is as if she is on the telephone relating a conversation to me. She asked for things to be clarified or repeated by the voice she is hearing. "Who is telling you this?" I asked. "Who is the voice you are hearing?"

"Your grandfather," she replied.

"Which one?" I asked, knowing that my maternal grandfather was still alive and well. "Your father's father," she replied.

"Describe him," I asked, imagining she would use me as a template and say something like, short, slim, compact. However, what she described was my grandfather perfectly. A big, broad, imposing gentleman, who made his presence felt as someone who took command as soon as he entered the room. A larger-than-life character with a soft side. She painted the picture as if he were there standing in front of me.

"What did he do for a living?" I asked. This would be the test of all tests. If she got close or even fairly close then my barriers would crash down, my beliefs would shatter and my whole understanding of what I thought I knew would be brought into question.

You see, as a Jewish boy growing up at the start of the 20th century in the East End, I would have expected her to say my grandfather was a tailor, a greengrocer – maybe a bookkeeper or doctor – but no.

She said "He was in the armed forces. He had an important job dealing with the things under the water." She had difficulty describing this perfectly, but I knew what she meant and with tears in my eyes I knew she was talking with my grandfather – Commander Morris Moss Bright, D.S.C RN, one of the first non-commissioned officers to rise through the ranks. What were the things under the water? They were mines because he was in charge of minesweepers.

Only he could have told her this – THIS WAS THE PROOF

I SOUGHT.

I asked what I should do, what did he want me to do – what next?

He said I should go straight away and see my parents, and then I would know what to do.

It was Saturday, and they were always out on a Saturday... no way would they be in. Denise said, "Phone them, they are in, because they are meant to be in!"

Of course, they were at home... they were meant to be at home, and neither of them could explain why they were at home other than it was a bright and sunny day and they thought they would stay at home in case I popped by!

So, I told them everything, and I immediately knew what to do. I had to get a divorce, I had to leave her and restart my life. It was only sometime later I realised what good advice my grandfather had given me. By telling the story, I could see the whole picture, like watching a film or reading a book. I knew how it should end, and I knew it was right.

Six months later, I met Deborah and two years later to the week we got married. This was no coincidence as the Jewish calendar only allows marriages to take place at certain times, and this was the only slot available to us at the time – now figure that out!

Over the years, Denise has often told us things she has heard or felt which cannot be explained, other than by her conversations with those we have loved and lost, who shelter us under their wings and guide us whenever possible.

PHILIP BRIGHT AND MEETING SIR SYDNEY SAMUELSON

The series of events which fall into place when Denise Jacobs is involved never ceases to amaze me. Is it that she knows the end goal and by some strange intervention she manages to be led there? Is it that she connects with people who connect with people? Or is it that the route has already been mapped out, and she knows who can open the doors at the right time? In any case, if it's meant to be then it will be!

One of the routes Denise was faced with was to get the film of her story off the page and into the world of producers, directors, cinematographers and studio heads. Denise and Michael, in weekly meetings with me and Deborah at our 'office' at a table in Concerto (a café in Westfield Shopping Centre) or at our home over egg on toast, had spent the best part of three years pulling together the incredible story of her life – her sixth sense, her trials and tribulations and produced what we all thought was a masterpiece screenplay. Well, that's what we thought!

Unlike the hundreds (maybe thousands) which do not even get a second glance, Denise knew this film would be – indeed, had to be – made, as the story was not only compelling, educational, thought-provoking, bizarre and (let's not forget) commercial, but it would change the way people thought for good.

"So, Philip, who do you know who can help us get this to the top?" she asked.

It was a few moments later that it dawned on me. Who better than Sir Sydney Samuelson, CBE, the government's first British Film Commissioner? A giant of the film industry, someone who would know everyone, give an honest opinion and best of all, an old family friend – I have known the Samuelson family all my life. My parents knew Sir Sydney and Lady Doris, while I grew up with his son Marc, attending Sunday school and birthday parties. We were four years old when we sat in their home in Hendon and were some of the first kids to be shown Thunderbirds – a work of genius.

So, it only took one phone call to set up the meeting with Denise, Michael and myself at Sir Sydney's home one Sunday morning.

Denise told him her story, what it meant to her, the toll it had taken over the years, the underlying message and how powerful it could be as a film, given the right producers and director.

Sir Sydney seemed absorbed, moved and intrigued by the whole story and agreed it needed amongst the best in the business to make it work and the one he felt would be right was Iain Smith – but the likelihood of getting him, even speaking with him was remote.

As I said at the beginning, Denise has a strange way of making things happen. How, we don't know, but all I can say is, it happens. Whilst I was not involved or present in what happened next, I do know that Denise got to speak to Iain Smith, via her friend Peter Jaques, who helped her take the next step. Is it coincidence, or is it destiny?

London
March 2018

DEBORAH BRIGHT

I first heard about Denise through my husband Philip when I started going out with him. He was going through a divorce and told me the most amazing and bizarre story of how Denise supported him through this traumatic situation with messages from 'the other side' – his deceased grandfather.

With his scientific mind, this was not something he would have believed; however, the information she gave him was so accurate and private that he believed her, and it helped him to choose how to move forward.

A most gentle, kind and caring person with not a mean bone in her body, over the past 27 years Denise has always been there not only as a friend, but in times of need and stress. There have been numerous occasions when I have contacted her, or, indeed, she has got in touch with me, because she has sensed her help was needed.

Having not seen Denise for a number of weeks, she suddenly telephoned and asked me directly if I was pregnant. It was the early stages of my pregnancy, and nobody had been told, so I asked her how she knew. She replied that a voice had popped into her head and told her.

Four and a half years ago, my father passed away. After the funeral, during the mourning period, there was an argument within the family with a lot of unpleasantness. This could have led to a split, and occurred at the saddest of times.

Denise, aware there was a problem, sensed she needed to come over to try and sort things out. Knowing that her own father was dying (he died less than two weeks later), this was a generous gesture. She sat down with us and started talking about my father as though he were with us in the room.

She said he was the polite, well turned-out, English gentleman we all knew and loved, always smartly dressed with shirt, jacket, tie and cufflinks – which was true. He would always look immaculate, and she particularly mentioned his smart, shiny black shoes. My father would polish and shine his shoes every Sunday night.

She could see the colour pale blue – this was literally within the week he died – and when the undertakers had taken my father, they asked if they could wrap him in the pale blue sheet he had been lying on. She further added that my father was comforting to her whilst she was planning her father's funeral, and he assured her that everything would be as she wished – and this turned out to be true.

My father also told her that he now knew that religion was man-made, something I found amazing as he had felt strongly about his faith. Bringing us together on that evening enabled our family to move on from the disagreement without causing a family split. I don't know how she managed, but it was quite remarkable and comforting during a time of deep sorrow.

In all the years we have known Denise, she has always reiterated her concern and anxiety over the worsening political situation globally and has expressed her concern over the increasing number of extremists and aggressors fighting in the name of faith.

It is quite extraordinary as well as disturbing to see how the things she has said and envisaged in those 27 years are materialising, and that the growing situation of evil and violence and nuclear threat is ever increasing. It is tangible to feel her desperation and despair over the malevolence and tragedy that may very well happen in the future.

I only hope that her messages are listened to and taken extremely seriously in order to eradicate the evil in the world.

London

March 2018

JONATHAN PEREZ

I had heard plenty of stories about Denise from my sister Deborah Bright. Many were scarcely believable and as someone who questions anything that isn't logical or cannot be proved empirically, there was a good deal of scepticism in my mind, even though the stories came from people who I trusted implicitly.

In February 2008 we met Denise and Michael at my niece Sarah's party. As we talked Denise began staring intently at my 16 year old daughter Mai. She turned to us and said that Mai was having issues and insisted that she had to speak with her as soon as possible.

The next day Denise came over and spent a couple of hours locked away with Mai. To this day we don't know what was discussed, but it's fair to say that this was the trigger which helped my daughter resolve many of the issues she was experiencing at the time.

Fast forward to September 2009. My wife and daughters decided that it was time we visited the newly opened Westfield Shopping Centre in Shepherds Bush for a bit of retail therapy and as Denise and Michael had planned a visit to Westfield on the same day, it was a perfect opportunity to meet up for a coffee, as we hadn't spoken for some time.

Michael and I left the girls to chat between themselves whilst we dropped into an intense conversation about football, enthusing over the wonderful start to the season our team Chelsea were having under new coach Carlo Ancelotti.

The girls chatted for a couple of minutes, before the subject switched to Annette's father. For Annette it was a sombre time as her father had passed away in early August following a long illness.

Denise asked Annette if her father had experienced a problem with his leg, because he wanted her wanted her to know that the pain had now gone. Back in the late 1950s, he had suffered a leg injury in an accident and he had suffered particularly in the final few years of his life. This was true, an old leg injury had given him a lot of trouble.

Denise then said to Annette that her father was telling her that they forgot his shoes in the hospital after he died. True enough. Whilst they had removed all of his belongings, after returning home they had discovered that his shoes were indeed missing; in all likelihood placed on a ledge under his bed when the room was being cleaned.

Annette felt guilty about something that had happened a couple of days before his death and Denise looked at Annette and said, your father is saying don't blame yourself, it's not your fault.

By this time Annette was in tears, this meant so much to her.

What had happened was that the nurse had come round to administer morphine to her father, to ease his pain. On this particular evening, he pleaded with the nurse not to give him the medicine. The nurse insisted, saying it would help him have a settled and painless night. He pleaded with his daughter saying, "Annetti, don't let them give me the medicine". But bowing to the superior knowledge of the medical staff, she said if it helps lessen your pain, then you should take the medicine.

Soon after receiving his dose of morphine, Annette's father fell asleep for the final time and after falling into a coma passed away a couple of days later.

After that Denise turned to Sapir, my younger daughter, and said, "Sapir, your grandfather is telling me to hug you tight, to pinch your cheeks for him and give you big kisses on the cheeks".

During the final weeks of his life, Annette had visited her father daily in hospital and each time as she left to go home, he would ask after all of his grandchildren. He would ask specifically about Sapir, who reminded him of Annette as a little girl. He would tell Annette to give Sapir a big hug, to pinch her cheeks and to give her big kisses on the cheeks.

I have to admit I was dumbfounded by all of this. I asked Denise how she could possibly have understood the messages since my father-in-law would not have spoken in English. Denise explained that the messages were not passed on in a spoken form, but she felt the messages in the same way that one experiences things that occur in a dream.

There is no logical explanation as to how Denise can provide such information and yet I believe in what she says. It seems as if there is a part of her brain which acts almost like an old fashioned radio receiver, twiddle the knobs and she tunes into a different frequency, the rest of us are unable to hear.

Denise does not gain financially or benefit in any way, other than her willingness to help people. When asked how I can believe in what she says, my reply would be that billions of people around the world are willing to believe in the power of a supreme being, something that is equally unprovable, so why should what Denise says be any less believable?

West London

January 2021

ANNETTE PEREZ

Having seen how effectively Denise identified issues with Mai and then provided solutions to most of her problems, I already believed that she seemed to possess some strange power.

About six weeks after my father passed away, we visited the new Westfield Shopping Centre and combined this with a chance to meet up with Denise and Michael, whom we hadn't seen in some time.

To say that I was blown away with what Denise told me would be an understatement. Apart from my daughters, I hadn't told anyone else the things that my father had said to me, yet here was someone passing on messages from beyond the grave. It was a bittersweet moment, and as sad and bereft as I felt at the loss of my father, somehow it gave me both belief and joy that he is still here. Knowing he is always with me and no longer suffering, even though I can't feel nor see him, is extremely comforting.

West London
January 2021

TERRY BILTON

To the readers of this book – I am Denise's older brother, and I can validate with 100% conviction that everything written in this book, even though it may be unbelievable to some, is totally true.

Over the years, I've had the privilege of receiving many unbelievable messages from her, and at the same time I have witnessed many occasions where Denise gave other people amazing messages. Early on, she proved that those messages were eerily accurate, and left me in no doubt that we are being watched from the other side, and that when we die, it's not the end of everything.

Half the time people were eager to listen to her, mesmerised by something being told to them that only they would know was accurate.

But, sadly... over the years, as her ability grew, and her reputation preceded her, a lot of other people would reject her attempt to give them messages, often reacting with a mixture of fear and scepticism.

Looking back, a lot of the people who rejected her admitted they believed that she could get messages, but were afraid she would tell them something bad, and would defensively tell Denise they didn't want to know the future or get messages from her.

I can categorically say I have never heard her give anyone bad news before... quite the opposite. It's almost always to give people help or hope, and comfort, when they are struggling through some crisis in life.

Denise and I had a little private phrase that we'd use when

we were discussing how her messages were received by people she tried to help...

They were either wearing the sunglasses... or not!

What we meant by that was this... people who were open to listening to her and were receptive to her messages... even eager to hear them... were the people who *weren't wearing any sunglasses*!

The other set of people, who rejected or dismissed her messages, we classed as the ones *wearing the sunglasses*!

One example was when she tried to give our mother a message from our brother Paul after he died, I think to make Mum feel that her son was no longer suffering the terrible effects from terminal brain cancer, but still there watching her.

She told Mum that in the morning, the day after he died, Paul was watching her pull clothes out of the washing machine, and all her tights were in a knot, and she tried to unravel them, but got so frustrated she lost her temper and started shredding them, ending up in tears.

Unfortunately, Mum's reaction was to loudly berate Denise, screaming, "If anyone could get messages from Paul, it would be *me*, and not *you*!"

Dad asked Mum if she had really got her tights in a knot and had lost her temper with them in the way Denise had described. Mum reluctantly admitted that she had. So even though Denise had given her a loving message from Paul that only Mum could validate as true, she rejected the whole thing. Our mum was one of the people who wore the very thick sunglasses.

Though I could spend hours describing some of the amazing and unbelievable messages that Denise gave me, one that has always stood out to me. It was when I was in my new hairdressing shop in Ft Lauderdale, Florida, trying to get it off the ground and make enough money to settle in America. I had opened the shop in early summer, thinking that would be the busiest time as it was in England, only to find out it was the opposite in South Florida – everyone goes away during the oppressive summer heat, and I was struggling to make a living.

I had called Denise in London to tell her I was thinking about dropping the whole thing and returning to England. She suddenly asked me if I knew anything about horses! She said that Celia was showing her a racehorse, and the message was to prove to me that everything would be OK. I just had to wait another three months, and the business would take off and I'd be fine.

I remember shaking my head and saying, "I don't know anything about racehorses," quietly thinking she had gone nuts. Feeling no better after my talk with her, I put the phone down, and within a few minutes, the door opened and a woman walked in and asked me if I could give her a cut and blow dry.

While I was shampooing her hair, I asked her what she did for a living, and she told me she trained racehorses – at which point my mouth dropped open in amazement.

As soon as I had finished her hair, I called Denise back and tell her what happened, and, as usual, she said, "There you go… everything is going to be OK".

By October of that year, people started coming back to South Florida, and my business took off – the messages were totally right.

From the early beginnings, when she first started to get her messages, Denise described in great detail the terrifying visions she had been shown of our world's total destruction through nuclear war, and how she was told she had been given the gift of being able to communicate with the deceased so she could warn everyone and try to stop it.

I have steadfastly supported Denise in her journey and, despite the sceptics, after all the evidence I have witnessed, I'm resolute in my intention to keep helping her, and I'm sad for those who reject her... they are missing out on so much!

My only hope is that there are enough people in the world who don't wear those damned sunglasses, and who will take Denise's warnings seriously and join forces to try to stop the few political leaders who control the world's fate.

Wisconsin, USA

June 2020

RICHARD V. COLAN MD., S.C.
CONSULTANT NEUROLOGIST

I have never met Denise Jacobs in person.

At about 60 Years of age, year 2000, I began experiencing mysterious attacks of explosive erratic heart rate, which would produce such disability through near fainting, that I could neither walk, nor drive. I would lie down, and or sit, and hope for early resolution. The spells lasted about 8 to 12 hours, and left me exhausted, progressively. At first, they were quite sporadic, occurring every few months, but after years, they begin to progress and take a toll on my energy and confidence. Work, exercise, active play had all become more problematic. A precise diagnosis finally arrived after considerable testing, of paroxysmal atrial fibrillation. Episodes increased over time to once weekly.

Initial trials of medication lead to difficult side effects, with only mild benefit.

One day in the late summer of 2009, I happened to be in the kitchen of my friend Terry Bilton. He was talking to his sister, Denise Jacobs, on his computer, as they did regularly. She was in London. We were in Racine, Wisconsin.

I walk past the computer, and heard Denise exclaim,

"Is that Richard? Terry, we can complete this later. I need to talk to him."

And she did talk to me. She told me that she had received messages that I was in a deteriorating state that I might be dying. She urged me to listen to her and follow her directions immediately. She told me that certain elements of my diet were combining to drive a deteriorating cardiac condition.

I presumed that she was surmising this from conversations with Terry.

I asked her how she would come to this conclusion, and she said, "You may not like this, but I'm getting messages from the next world that are clearly aimed at you. She was quite adamant. She said to start by discontinuing these food elements; that at first it would really suck, and after about three days, I would begin experiencing benefits.

As a western trained physician, I had my doubts about any of this, but thought it wouldn't hurt to try it. The results were immediate. Instead of having sustained attacks once weekly, with an entire day down with disability, I experienced no more than one or two brief episodes in the next six months with no disability. In addition, there are other benefits, improved energy, gradual appropriate weight loss, and better sleep. I was able to exercise again, got back to regular tennis, and physical activity, benefits which have persisted to this day.

I am eternally grateful to Denise, and her bold determination to deliver these messages to me. At the time, it was quite difficult to believe the basis of her information; applying it has immensely improved and possibly saved my life. She never asked for anything in return.

Wisconsin, USA
March 2018

ASSERS - A NOTE FROM CARL FLEMING

Assers is documented to 1453 and traceable to 1279 – a truly ancient property.

It was to be another 40 years before Columbus even set sail to discover America and 50 years before Leonardo da Vinci painted the Mona Lisa, and Assers was already built!

According to the Listed Building department of Chelmsford City Council, a William Asser and his family lived in Good Easter in 1279.

Asserdom was a licence handed out by the church to individuals to allow them to clear woodland to make agricultural land. Hence, the people with these licences became known as 'Assers', in the same way that blacksmiths became 'smithies' or 'smiths'.

It may have been part of a Hall House, but before that it was quite small with animals downstairs and people living upstairs. It has a lovely original mullioned window that is very ancient. It is indeed a piece of English history. I feel quite honoured to have owned and restored it for future generations. I have left my mark.

MICHAEL JACOBS

Jonathan Blair's text arrived on May 15th, 2020:

JONATHAN
Jeff has gone...

MICHAEL
Oh no.... I'm so gutted

That was how we heard my best friend had died. I had known him since 1963; longer than I had known anyone in my life, including Denise.

Jeff had Progressive Supranuclear Palsy (PSP), and he had been unable to communicate, swallow food or walk. I was inconsolable. My best friend had died, and I would never see or speak to him again.

It was over dinner that night when Denise stepped in. "Jeff's here, Michael. He's fine now, and very happy. He wants me to remind you of his yellow socks, and also how you both used to enjoy scrambled eggs at 3am."

I began to sob, again. "That's got to be Jeff! We spent many a Saturday night after being out on the town, having a 3am breakfast of scrambled eggs at the Cavendish Hotel off Piccadilly. It seems like a million years ago."

After his messages to me, Jeff asked Denise to phone his nephew Jonathan. "Jeff's back, well and happy," she told him. "He wants to say a big thank you to you and Neil for everything you did to help him whilst he was so ill."

The following day, Denise was told to phone Jeff's wife,

Elaine. "Jeff wants to say sorry to you for being so ill, and he said to tell you that you pulled the short straw with him and his health. He loves you very much and you have been a wonderful wife for putting up with him. He wants you to know that he didn't suffer any pain." Elaine asked who was with him now, and Denise replied, "He's well and with his parents, family and friends."

Because Denise is the only one with the ability, she was being used as a telephone by Jeff to talk to those he loved. It was magical. It can prove so helpful to those who are in pain, after losing a loved one, to learn the deceased are still around but in another dimension. A place we all go to after our allotted time is up. Denise calls it 'going home'.

Middlesex

May 2020

AND FINALLY... HIS HONOUR JUDGE CHARLES LAMBERT PURLE QC

February 9th, 1947 – May 5th, 2018
Extracted from emails and texts I received from Charles...

> *Alive and well. Pleased to hear the script has made it to the next stage. I am happy to review the legal aspects of it. The story hasn't become any less topical. This picture is me as a Judge, which is slightly different from the barrister and QC gear.*

> *See you at the premier, if not before. Seeing Swan Lake for the umpteenth time next Christmas with my grandchildren! Now tired and retired, but well!*

> *Must see you soon. Good luck. Will be in touch (promise!) xxx*

I was in the middle of cooking when I had the feeling something was amiss with Charles. I turned off the hob and, wondering why, I found myself walking over to my laptop. I Googled his name, something I'd never done before. That was when I discovered he had left this world.

I was shocked, saddened and sobbed at the news. He was so enthusiastic about the story being told and amused at the thought of seeing himself being depicted in a book and on the big screen. As I sat there trying to take in the news, I heard his voice, "I told you I'd be in touch!" I burst out laughing. "Charles, you kept your promise to me!"

He was standing beside me in the conservatory, without the need for his wheelchair – no longer paralysed from the waist down.

Grinning that huge cheery grin of his he patted me on the back and in that inimitable voice of his said, "Well done, my wonderfully weird woman. I'm proud of you."

ACKNOWLEDGMENTS

This book would not have been possible without the help of many talented and generous people.

When the idea of writing it was first suggested one hot summer night in the Mediterranean by the extraordinary Grahame Sutton, I was terrified at the idea, but you were right Grahame. Thank-you for believing in me all the way.

Step forward the exceptionally talented Caro Handley, showing all the patience in the world to me and who not only brought my story to life but became a great friend in the process. Thank you for being you, Caro.

To achieve your goal in life takes strength, determination, and singlemindedness. It also needs the tolerance and love of special people in your life. Without the wonderful support of my long-suffering husband, Michael, who discovered a new room in the house (the kitchen) and my darling son, Daniel, who I love to the moon and back, there would be no book. Also, my wonderful brother Terry who has been steadfast and always there for me no matter what. Thank you, boys.

Creating this story was made so much easier with the help of Michael's meticulous diaries which he has kept for the past forty years, confirming all the events that took place. Nick Montgomery created a brilliant document from those diaries that could be cross-referenced. Nick, your work of art was used constantly by both Caro and me, for which I thank you with all my heart.

Thanks also to Anthony Harvison, my PR guru: you have been so supportive. And to website wizard Marc Crane, who created the *Red Amaryllis* website and logo. I'd also like to thank Sam Rumbelow for your excellent advice and assistance and Christine Meldon Photography for yours, too.

My mentor, film producer Iain Smith, also deserves a special mention. From the very beginning you gave me the courage to put pen to paper and showed such patience when trying to teach me how to write a screenplay. Enormous thanks too, to film producer Peter Jaques, for all your advice and encouragement. Another special mention goes to Jonny Persey and the Met Film School of London for your advice and support in teaching me how to write for the screen and to Sir Sidney Samuelson who recognised the remarkable story that this is. Many thanks to the talented commercial entertainment lawyer Jonathan Blair; you never stopped showing faith in me and always got it right. Thanks also to Carola Ash, Neil Blair and Andrew Lownie for your valuable knowledge and input. My gratitude goes to multi-talented actor Jonathan Kydd for your wonderful voiceover on two separate videos. Thanks also goes to Daniel Jacobs for your beautiful music on the video and your creative input and invaluable assistance throughout.

I am grateful for help of so many people for your guidance,

belief and support –especially the Bright family, Deborah and Philip not only for your patience reading through so many manuscripts but for helping in so many other ways. Also, to Sarah and Aaron for always being there too. Thanks to the magnificent Jonathan Perez for the chapter cover sheets, to Bern Thompson for your editing, to Carrol Moore for checking everything out so many times, to Claire Handley and Teo Handley for your advice. Special thanks to the wonderful Anthony Fiducia, my now-retired lawyer, and to the late darling His Honour Charles Purle QC.

I am eternally grateful to all those witnesses who not only allowed me to recount their personal stories but who were also prepared to put their names to them to underline the veracity of my messages. Thank you to my brother Terry Bilton, Anthony Fiducia, Nick Montgomery, Liz Longley, Philip and Deborah Bright, Sir Sydney Samuelson, Annette and Jonathan Perez, Bill and Carole Blass, Sue Rule, Marilyn Macaluso, Janet West and of course, John Cradduck of 'The Flower Stall' Uxbridge, not only for your story but for your beautiful bunches of red amaryllises, sent via you from my late parents, which gave me the title for the book.

If I have left anyone out, I am truly sorry, but it does not diminish my eternal gratitude for your selflessness in helping me to tell my extraordinary story.

And thanks to you, dear reader. Although I don't know you personally, I hope my story gives you comfort in knowing that the next dimension exists and is interlinked with ours in a miraculous way. I hope you have accepted the proof that those you love have never left you but are with you, looking on at all you do. And if you are still unsure, I hope that you have been persuaded to become more open-minded and to reconsider your beliefs. And for you, if you are a world leader, I hope you take inspiration and act upon Paul's warning. Not only is our future in your hands, but your own future and that of your family too. It's up to you to decide which route you wish to take.

Finally, my biggest thanks must go to two very special people for always being with me, no matter what.

Celia Jacobs

(1912 – 1980)

Paul Stephen Bilton

(1958 – 1992)

Thank you both, I hope I have done justice to the story you wanted me to tell and the warning you want me to give.